COMMUNICATION ESSENTIALS:

A Sell-Abration

by

Ronni Burns

D1196349

ISBN: 1-4196-7522-2
ISBN-13: 978-1419675225

Visit www.booksurge.com to order additional copies.

CONTENTS

Ronni Burns is an expert in the art of persuasion. She travels the country educating professionals on how to increase the effectiveness of their communication. This book is the first time she shares her philosophy that *"life is just one big sell-abration!"*

Communication essentials includes being aware of what you say and *how* you say it. Each person emits a constant stream of clues about how to reach them with maximum effect. The complete communicator listens with all senses and tailors each communication.

Complete communicators pay special attention to gender differences, and *cross address* when speaking to someone of the opposite sex.

Finally, complete communication is about developing and using your sense of humor, your intuition, and your powers of creative thinking.

This chapter discusses many dos and don'ts of verbal communication. It includes a section on the art of persuasion and advice on self-talk.

This chapter addresses the actual sound of your voice and how to improve it.

Listening involves far more than your ears. This chapter advises that you *listen with all of your senses*, which puts you in a position to not only hear the speaker's message, but to empathize with them.

Body language can often undermine words. Pay attention to the non-verbal language patterns of others in order to decode what they are really saying.

Humor
Intuition
Creative Thinking

The *invisibles* are parts of behavior that most people don't pay much conscious attention to. But neglecting them means allowing potentially powerful allies to lie dormant. Cultivating them can give you an edge in your business and personal lives.

Gender differences have been a popular topic of conversation in every industry for about a decade. This chapter addresses the need for sensitivity and *cross addressing*, and discusses some of the most problematic gender related problems in communication.

It is recommended that you keep a notebook chroni-
cling your progress. This chapter contains excerpts
from the notebooks of a husband and wife.

INTRODUCTION

I wrote this book because I wanted to demystify how we communicate and offer tools and techniques you could use to help you get more of what you want. I wanted to share my thoughts and experiences about how and why people make the decisions they make. You know, explain a process that is largely unconscious. I wanted to explain how, with only limited information, we all can learn to predict how people are going to behave and react.

I wanted to let you in on the secrets of how people are persuaded, influenced, and sold. And I wanted to do this in a humorous way so you would relate to it and remember it. My motto has always been: Why be boring if you can be entertaining? Why overcomplicate things when you can give practical wisdom with entertaining twists?

I wanted to help you learn to trust, nurture, and use your intuition. You might be amazed by how helpful it can be. I wanted to show you how important it is to develop your sense of humor and hone your thinking skills, they both aid in dealing with adversity. Above all, I wanted to write a book that everyone could find themselves in, and that everyone could use. It is easy to improve yourself and make some changes when it is made simple and you see how beneficial the payoffs can be.

At the conclusion of one of my speeches someone wrote in a critique that "Ronni offers polished common sense." Thanks. I like that. This is what I offer to you in this book.

So enough about you... how about me?

Well, my name is Ronni Burns, and my favorite four letter word is "sell." But it wasn't always that way.

In fact, when I was just starting my career someone I greatly respect said to me, "Ronni, you would be a natural in sales, have you considered it?"

"What?" I snapped. "You mean you think I should sell make-up in a department store?" Little did I know that the whole world was one big *sellabration*. I had a lot to learn.

1

Each day, and probably several times each day, most of us are selling something: an idea, a recommendation, ourselves. Whether or not you consider yourself a member of a sales force is a matter of semantics and preference. But the reality is that we all have ideas that we are trying to get others to go along with, wittingly or otherwise. It is rare to get to quote Joseph Stalin, but it is alleged that he said, "You get more with a smile and a gun than you do with just a smile." I'd much rather skip the gun and have a willing subject.

So, if you accept the premise that we all are selling all of the time, why not do it well, or better?

The Need for Communication Essentials

Formal education teaches us a lot about humans as a species. We learn about how the human body works and what it can do. We know that we can communicate using verbal language as well as nonverbal language. We learn that we have instincts; some, we are sure about (survival), others, we endlessly debate. Is there a maternal instinct? Is communication an instinct? But regardless of whether communication is an instinct, most of us still have to learn about its myriad variables and then we have to practice how to do it *effectively*. Most of us have to be taught how to operate *ourselves* so that we are understood and we understand others.

Helping you learn how to operate your *self* is my objective for this book. The complete communicator uses the entire *self* to maximize each communication and considers the other person's entire *self* as well. The complete communicator is not intimidated by the idea of sales, because it is merely a word that describes a situation where the knowledge of the self and of others makes it possible for productive communication and mutual benefit to occur.

And while your knowledge of yourself is greater than your knowledge of others, you can tell a lot about a person by the clues they give you. Complete communicators know that we all continuously give off clues about who we are and how we want to be treated. The way we stand, the way we speak, the way we listen, the things we find funny, and even our gender, send signals to those around us about how we want to be treated.

Am I the only one who sees these connections?

I think it's safe to say that most people see the connectedness in what we say, how we say it, and what we look like when we are saying it. Most people are aware that, in addition to listening, these are the main aspects of communication. Talking about communication and some of its important factors has been a trend in motivational speaking and in training for about a decade.

2

But I see the four elements typically discussed as an incomplete description of what is involved in communication. I see them as the *results* of what happens in communication. After all, you say what you say because you had a thought or a feeling internally. And those thoughts and feelings are influenced by gender and by what I like to call *invisibles*. Your verbal and nonverbal communication (your external self) is largely affected by your intuition, your sense of humor, and your creative thinking (your internal self). The *invisibles* profoundly influence what you say, how you say it, how you look, and how you listen. They influence them because they influence *you*.

What do I know?

My education and training at the University of Pennsylvania combined with my graduate training in social work and communications gave me reams of theoretical knowledge and hours of experiential knowledge about human communication. They were my foundation. Fortunately, I was in a position to test what I had learned during my formal education by spending two decades working with sales professionals in various industries. And I was in a position to delve into the rarely examined area of humor in my own extracurricular way, as a stand-up comic.

I concentrated my efforts as a consultant in the financial services industry, with people who were dedicated to improving the relationships they had with their clients. Relationship-based selling was becoming the popular mode of doing business because it worked—and Wall Street in the 1980s was no exception. I began like many others in the field, discussing ways to optimize your relationships by examining verbal and nonverbal communication.

I ventured into researching humor, intuition, creative thinking, and gender because I believed that the typical discussions about relationships and their communication were missing those vital elements. Gender eventually entered the mainstream discussion about communication (and with a vengeance), but *the invisibles* remained neglected. It was my examination and integration of *the invisibles* that made what I offer my clients a bit different from the many other consultants in my field. I gave them the theory and practice that helped them become better at presenting, persuading, and closing, but it was *the invisibles* that helped them learn how to overcome adversity in all kinds of relationships. Mastering their own internal invisibles gave them the edge they needed.

They were becoming better salespeople, yes. But more important was that they were becoming better *people*. They were able to say what they mean and mean what they say. They realized that the message in any communication is the one that the listener heard—not the one they were so sure that they transmitted. They worked on using

3

their thoughts, their bodies, their feelings—their *selves*—to send the messages they intended to send, listen with all of their senses, and raise the level of their conversations. They were becoming *complete communicators*. You can too.

CHAPTER ONE

Communication Essentials

When I began this project I asked myself the same question I ask the people who attend my seminars on persuasion and selling: What is your objective for this communication? This is a key question and I suggest you borrow it off the page right now. Use it whenever you are about to, or preparing to, communicate with anybody about anything.

When you prepare for communication it will save you a lot of time in the long run, and help you to maintain your sanity. When you try to define what it is you want to accomplish, you begin to organize your thoughts toward achieving a goal. That goal is: How do I want the other person to feel, think, or act, as a result of me opening my mouth and speaking. And how will my appearance and gestures support that goal? Once a communication situation is framed this way it is much easier to formulate your plan.

This goal of this communication—this book—has five parts:

1) to help you realize that your words, your gestures, your tone, and the way you listen, affect others and ultimately determine the outcome of each conversation you have;
2) to help you establish your proficiency at those elements and then help you hone your skills;
3) to help you locate your intuition and become comfortable with its workings and help you define and develop your sense of humor and your critical thinking abilities;
4) to help you understand the role of gender in communication; and
5) to help you learn how to interpret the verbal and nonverbal language of others, based on your increasing knowledge of the aspects of complete communication.

Communication Essentials is about you and how you express yourself and how you interpret the verbal and nonverbal expressions of others. It is about dealing with others in a way that respects their thoughts and their feelings, and hears their messages while sending messages that match your intent.

Patterns and Rules

Regardless of where you are, whom you are speaking to, and what your subject is, you have to deal with people. People, as we all have observed (and some of us do so for a living) are predictable creatures who have created procedures and rules for many of life's circumstances. Some of our standard operating procedures have rules that were established for a reason, such as the rules of our legal system. And some have evolved and spread and seem to have no real function, yet we conform nevertheless.

For example, Mikki Williams, a public speaker, talks about Elevator Rules. You know, the first person in goes to the back left, the next one goes to the back right, then the front left, followed by the front right, and finally the center. And what's the one thing you never do in an elevator? Turn around. Why? Because that's the way it's done. In my opinion, that is as good an answer as "Because I'm your mother."

Our rules are only effective as long as we follow them and whether or not we do is a matter of choice. Part of the essentials of Communication is knowing what the rules are, then knowing when to bend, blend, or break them to increase the success of your communication and alter its once predictable outcome. Let me illustrate with a hypothetical. Suppose you are caught speeding by a policeman. What is the ordinary chain of events? Perhaps something like this...

> *You hear loud sirens, your heart races, you frantically construct an argument in your head, and perhaps even work up some tears (if you're female and that kind of thing works for you). For a brief couple of seconds you are involved in a chase (or so it seems, until you can find a place to pull over). Several moments later you look up and see a belt buckle and continue moving your eyes up until you see those regulation mirrored sunglasses and you say (insert your favorite excuse here).*
>
> *This is a predictable pattern, and in order to change the predictable outcome, you have to change the dance. Ordinarily, the officer attacks and you defend. The officer says you were speeding and you are shocked at the accusation and offer some excuse, which he mutters to himself is #305, or "Hmm, that's a new one."*
>
> *Next time, try this: "Officer, thank you so much for stopping me. Why, I could have hurt myself, or worse,*

6

*I could have hurt someone else. Can I write a letter to
your boss commending you on a job well done? You
may have saved my life and the lives of others, and
once again I humbly thank you.*"

Though this may appear to be a Jedi-mind trick, what it does is
change the predictable course of the communication, which just might
change its outcome. When you change your part the officer can't play
his usual part. (Of course now I've got to stick to the speed limit
because I'll never get away with this reaction again now that you will
all use it.)

Patterns and Sales

Successful salespeople have discovered that most conversations
have patterns. They are aware of the different permutations of conversations based on which objections are raised, when they are raised,
and how they are raised. They listen to their intuition. They listen
also with their eyes: attending to the way their prospect is standing,
sitting, and gesturing, and how his eyes move. They look for patterns
in all of those elements in an effort to decode the real message. They
mirror their prospect. (More about this later but for now it's enough to
know that we tend to feel comfortable with people who are like us.)
They help the prospect make decisions by raising objections before
their prospect does. They know what they want, they find out what
the prospect wants, and then they create a win/win situation. In order
to accomplish this there must *be* complete communication.

Good salespeople let the other person lead the dance. They enjoy
helping others get what they want and need. Good salespeople learn
from others because they know they have much to learn and they are
receptive. They strengthen relationships through the way they communicate.

Sales and Life

I recall speaking in front of a hundred or so of the top producers
of one of the largest Wall Street firms and thinking: "Why do I talk
only to brokers?" Sure, it's the industry I know best, but why is what
they do from 8 A.M. to 6 P.M. different from what they do when they go
home to their families? I voiced this concern to the client who had
hired me and just for fun I threw in a free session for the spouses of
the participants. The session was very well received and convinced me
that learning the way of the successful salesperson is something
everyone can benefit from.

Shortly thereafter my young son approached me. Clearly there
was something important on his mind, but being my son taught him
that his crucial moment might not be well received if I wasn't ready

for it. He looked me in the eye and inquired, "Is this a good time to talk, Mom, or would Friday at 3:00 P.M. be better for you?" I'm not kidding. When I say everyone can benefit from good communication skills I mean everyone.

Everything in its place

Human beings seem to have a need to categorize and compartmentalize. We like to put things in what we think are their appropriate boxes. All is right with the world when things are properly boxed. We are comforted by the thought that things are in their right place, at least according to how we judge where they should be.

Likewise, we get upset when faced with square pegs, or worse, things that can fit into two boxes yet neither is a snug fit. Then there are the times when something is in the box already, like when we have made a hasty conclusion and are forced to find some evidence, or concoct some evidence, to make the box fit.

There is so much information available to us that developing good selective attention skills is necessary for survival. And that survival skill is cultivated at home as well as in school, from a very young age. Imagine each one of twenty students in a class thinking *I wonder why* and then asking the teacher *why?* The school day would never end and the class most certainly wouldn't get through the required curriculum.

A concrete example of our self-imposed limitations and our need to categorize is something that I have observed as a parent. When I was in grammar school the main subjects we learned about were math, science, history, and English. I always wondered why manufacturers kept producing five subject notebooks when there were really only four subjects. Was the last section to be split between art and music? Did that mean they were less important or not *real* subjects? I was somehow taught English as if it existed in a vacuum, and then when I wrote my history papers I didn't have to worry about my spelling and punctuation because that stuff was for English class. So did that mean that I had to speak correctly only when my English teacher was listening? What purpose did the boundaries serve?

Fortunately for children today, in the interim decades there was a revolution in education and the upshot was that educators realized that life is truly an interdisciplinary experience. Science and math are closely related. And music is really math. English, as it turns out, isn't really anything because it is everything.

The Casualty of Everything in its Place

When you spend so much mental energy categorizing and you make categorization your primary strategy for processing new information, you are priming yourself to overlook the interconnectedness of what is around you. Consider what you do for a living. You probably have a name for it: a label. There's nothing wrong with that, as it helps you let others know in an instant what you get paid to do. But it is not who you are and I bet you do lots of other things during your workday.

We are not all firemen, yet we all put out fires of different types everyday. We are not all healers, yet we all heal with our words and our deeds. We are not all attorneys, yet we have all staunchly and systematically defended our ideas and/or prosecuted others (and how many of us, when things get adversarial, have said, "Will the witness just answer the question," or "Nothing further, you may step down"). We are not all salespeople, yet we all try to persuade others to willingly go along with our ideas.

The Value of Good Persuasion Skills

I have read many books on persuasion and given countless lectures on the topic in addition to spending years as a salesperson and a spokesperson. I learned about which words to use and which ones to avoid if I wanted to maximize the probability that my prospects would respond the way I wanted them to (i.e., laugh, take notes, buy another seminar, laugh some more). I also ventured into the realm of nonverbal communication, studying what we are saying when we aren't saying anything with words. I spent a lot of time observing others. I studied the principles of proxemics, which is how relationships are affected by where people are and *how they are being* in their physical space. I have been trained by masters on how to persuade using nonverbal cues and I have trained others how to do so.

The Limits of Persuasion

The art of persuasion and influence has been my vocation and my avocation for most of my adult life. For me, it was a challenge and a game wherein I knew that if I had to, I could convince the proverbial Eskimo that he was in need of snow. And not just any snow—my top quality snow that was in limited supply. I'd say my skill at persuasion was a smashing success. Somewhere along the line, though, the idea of persuasion seemed to become skewed and lose a bit of humanity.

I was feeling that something important was missing when I was in Persuasion Mode. And it was the same thing I had observed in and heard about from many salespeople over the years. The problem stemmed from the reality that many of us were full of techniques and strategies and obviously had attended a lot of the same workshops. Consequently, many of us overemphasized the trend du jour, whether it was "the most effective gestures," "power words," or "eye contact for successful closing."

Our goal was to convince the other person that he really wanted what *we really wanted him to want*. It usually worked. He got stuff and we got paid. I'd like to say that we were misguided, but in fact we were guiding ourselves in the direction of a specific goal: the sale. And some of us were able to reach it time after time. But all the while we were neglecting a very important, very *vital* part of the equation: the prospect. It is only in retrospect that it is so clear that we simply were aiming for the wrong goal. A redefinition of our goal and of persuasion was in order.

The real goal is the win/win outcome and the way to get there is through *complete communication.* The win/win, as I will discuss later, is not synonymous with compromise. In a compromise both sides give up something and don't get exactly what they want. In a win/win both sides get what they want.

Communication Essentials—A Sellabration of Awareness

At work and in our personal lives, we should try to be the best we can be as individuals. I'm sure I won't get any disagreement about that. In interpersonal communication, the best we can be involves making certain the impression we give and the message we send are consistent and honest. We want our thoughts, words, and actions to be consistent with one another.

Fortunately, there is much literature on how you should sound and look while you are using what experts agree is the most effective vocabulary for a given situation. I have found however, that what my clients need most is one simple guide that explains the do's and don'ts of these aspects of successful communication, and that also includes the more subtle, more invisible pieces of the communication puzzle. The *invisibles* are aspects of our being that we don't ever really see or hear. They live inside of you, but glimpses can be seen from the outside. For instance, creative thinking is not something you can see or put your finger on. But your proficiency at it will affect what you do and say (which, in contrast, is easily identifiable).

I composed this book in order to decode, demystify, and share my thoughts and experiences about what makes communication in all kinds of relationships successful. The complete communicator, as I define it, is a person who is mindful of:

- What he is saying
- How he is saying it
- How he listens
- What the normal nonverbal communication is saying
- The invisible elements of humor, intuition, and creative thinking
- The role of gender in communication

The emphasis with all of these variables is on cultivating a higher degree of awareness of what is occurring. It is the complete communicator's awareness of how all of these elements interact that gives him an edge. The complete communicator's constant assessment and re-assessment of how he is being received as well as what he believes he is transmitting will help him achieve his desired outcome.

My Intention

My intention is to first isolate your communication muscles and then strengthen them and get them to work together to express *your* intentions. I hope also to help you develop the kind of x-ray vision that will enable you to see through to the heart of any communication problem. And I want your ears to be able to hear what is not being said. I want you to realize that if you do things differently, break free from patterns, experience life from an angle that is not typical for you, I promise you that you will enjoy yourself more, laugh (at yourself) more, and increase your awareness of yourself and everyone around you. You will become what I like to call a *social detective* rather than a passive observer.

Communication is both an art and a science. It is a science because it has rules and it is an art because you need to know when, where, and how to apply those rules for maximum effect. And remember, you also have to know when to bend, blend, or even break the rules. The complete communicator is a person who is comfortable in his own skin, knows what to attend to, and knows how he is perceived. He knows what they want to say and to mean, and his being and his words are consistent with that message. *His intentions are the same as what is received by his listener.* This is the optimal situation. But it is not as common as it could be.

What is your most common experience in conversation?

A conversation is supposed to consist of at least two people exchanging ideas. It is supposed to involve speaking, listening, perceiving, and feeling, by both parties. However, I am certain you are familiar with several types of pseudoconversations which are more like two people masquerading as participants in a conversation. The ones I have observed most often are: *the simultaneous monologue, the debate, and the lecture.*

The *simultaneous monologue* is the subtle phenomenon wherein each participant has an agenda established long before the actual meeting and nothing the other person says is going to change what they have decided they are going to say or think. Naturally, there is no listening during simultaneous monologues, except when scouting for the opportune moment to mention the next profundity. Nor is there much perceiving because how the other person really feels is of little consequence when you have an established plan of verbal exposition. Furthermore, when you have already decided what you are going to say you are probably not planning on doing much listening, so you are unlikely to develop an emotional reaction that has not been orchestrated in advance.

Emotions do get triggered in *debates* where each participant considers the other an adversary. The motivation of both sides is to attack the other side and prove its thoughts to be wrong. In fact, what often happens is that not only are the thoughts attacked, but that sentiment somehow gets personalized and expanded to mean that *the person having the thoughts* is wrong, or *there is something wrong with them*. Obviously, there is no real winner in a pseudoconversation such as this and feelings invariably get hurt along the way.

Another common pseudoconversation, particularly between men and women, is *the lecture* that is given to an audience of one. The speaker/lecturer in this situation does not consider the listener's thoughts or feelings, so there is no actual exchange. The listener feels unimportant and resentful, and alleges that the speaker is a selfish person with an exaggerated sense of self-importance. However, the fault does not lie solely on the lecturer, particularly if the listener isn't really listening. It is fairly easy to become a lecturer when your listener isn't participating. Listeners, I will discuss, have an enormous amount of responsibility and have as much power to control the structure of the conversation as speakers do. And because men and women tend to have different conversational styles, including different listening styles, honing your listening skills is probably the most important thing you can do to improve your communication.

Think about the typical course of your conversations. Is there a pattern? How do you feel when you think about the majority of your verbal exchanges? How do you think the people with whom you speak would respond to the same questions? What box would they put you in: good listener, attacker, blamer, or maybe bore that goes on and on about themselves? Are your conversations with men different from those with women? Are you different when you are speaking with one person than you are when you are with a group? If so, how are you different? Are you perceived differently?

How to use this book:

Joe Spoelstra, a popular motivational speaker who spent over twenty years in the management end of professional basketball, wrote a short, yet powerful book called *Success is Just One Wish Away*. The main character is a large, Japanese-looking genie named Darrell who has a Brooklyn accent, but I won't reveal anything more about the story. I don't think I'm giving away too much by telling you that part of Spoelstra's plan for success in life is to decide what you need to improve in your life, plan out the necessary steps, write them down, and shoot to conquer a couple every month or two. I'm sure you've heard this before, it's not groundbreaking stuff. It's a great story though, and I especially like the way Spoelstra talks about implementing your list of things you need to do. "Improving or initiating something new for most people is usually *random* and *infrequent* and often *unplanned*. What we're talking about is *not random*, it's *not infrequent*, it's *not unplanned*" (115).

I suggest you use *Communication Essentials* as a diagnostic tool that will help you make a map of what you need to improve. This book will help you improve your communication in a way that is not random or unplanned. Each of the following five chapters deals with a different aspect of communication. I recommend keeping a five-subject notebook next to you while you are reading so you can take notes, and write comments and questions (all of which I'd be happy to answer if I can).

Most important is that in each of these chapters I included **self discovery** exercises. After all, this book is about developing an awareness of the way you communicate. The Self Discovery is the time for you to evaluate your own aptitude at each aspect of communication, as best you can, with the help of a microcassette recorder and a trusted friend. The microcassette recorder is one of my favorite tools. Once you get accustomed to carrying it around (which may take a day or two) you will be amazed at what you hear when you play back your tapes. Most people have no idea how they really sound to others. The trusted friend is a buddy of yours whose aid you will enlist to give you an idea of how others receive you, not just how you sound. Your buddy can tell you things that aren't necessarily detectable in conversation. I suggest recording all of the observations you and your buddy have in your notebook.

When you are finished assessing your ability in each of the areas I address you will have a better idea of where you are now, you will have established your baseline. You will know about your competence regarding:

- what you say
- the words you use
- how well you listen
- what you look like when you are speaking and listening
- how your sense of humor comes across
- how you interpret intuitive signs
- how you think

Your assessment of where you are is the first leg of your journey toward the esentials of communication. If you haven't already, you should articulate on paper, precisely what it is you want to be in your relationships—*how* you want to be in your relationships. How do you want to feel about yourself? How do you want to feel about other people? What do you want others to think and say of you as a communicator and as a person? How do you want to be able to deal with adversity? The more details, the more adjectives and adverbs you use in your list, the more helpful it will be. After all, only when you know where you want to go, will you be able to effectively use the information about where you are. Your map will emerge before your eyes once you are clear about these two sets of information.

Summary

- Communication Essentials involve:

    1. What you say
    2. How you say it
    3. Your listening style and skills
    4. Your nonverbal communication of gestures and body language
    5. Your mastery of *the invisibles* (your intuition, your sense of humor, and your creative thinking)
    6. The influence that gender has on communication

- There are unspoken rules in interpersonal communication that allow you to predict how others will behave and respond. Mastery of those rules helps the complete communicator help others get what they want.
- Good salespeople are good because they tend to be complete communicators. They reach far beyond traditional sales techniques and realize that success with the subtle art of persuasion begins with knowing and maximizing *yourself*. And once you know your *self*, it is easier to understand others and what they want and need.
- *Communication Essentials* will help you determine your proficiency at all of the elements of communication, both visible and invisible, so you can begin your journey toward optimization of your *self*.

14

CHAPTER TWO

What You Say

There was a beautiful dog in a pound. On his cage, just like the cages of the other dogs, whether beautiful or mangy, there was a nametag. His name was Killer. People would come to the pound and move quickly past the cage, looking anxious. One morning, one of the workers replaced the nametag with one that said "Baby." "AWWWW, how precious," people would say as they walked by, always putting a finger or two in the cage to try to pet his nose. Baby was adopted shortly thereafter.

—True Story

The most often cited study regarding the impact of communication is by Albert Mehrabian of the University of Southern California and was published in 1971. Mehrabian defined and scientifically measured the relationship between three essential components of a personal presentation in determining our believability. He found that words account for only 7 percent of the impact of our message, while our tone of voice accounts for 38 percent, and our nonverbal communication accounts for 55 percent.

In other words, 55 percent of your effectiveness as a speaker is determined by your visual expression, including how you look (your grooming, clothes, and accessories), your gestures, your posture, your movement, your facial expression, and your eye contact. The actual sound of your voice is 38 percent responsible for whatever impact you have, and the words that you use account for a mere 7 percent.

A mere 7 percent?

Some would say that if your words account for only 7 percent of your message, your time is best spent on improving your appearance and your nonverbal communication. And there are plenty of books to read and courses to take on how to create the kind of nonverbal presence that is most effective for particular situations. I will give you

15

some advice in Chapter Five: What You Look Like. My take on the 7 percent, however, is that it means you have less of a margin for error with the words you use, so you should be as careful and deliberate as possible.

In addition, it is a lot easier to control your words than your nonverbal communication, because most of the latter is unconscious. Finally, because we cannot control the words of others even as parents and teachers (although we can influence them), our time is probably better spent examining how we speak and what messages we are sending to others.

Maximizing Your 7 percent

Communicating what you intend to communicate and getting confirmation that your message has been received and understood as you intended is not a simple process. Even if you believe that you have used words that precisely describe what it is you want to say, there is no guarantee that your listener is going to get the message you are so certain you sent. Why? Because all human beings attach meaning to words based on their past experiences.

Each individual has words that are especially "loaded" for them. Due to the association of emotion and/or memory of a prior experience, a word that could be neutral and simply explanatory or descriptive to one person can represent something completely different to someone else. And this semantic challenge is exacerbated by the fact that even if you have known someone for a long while and have been attentive to what triggers them, you probably don't know the whole story. A little knowledge can be a dangerous thing because it leads to assumptions that can get you into trouble. You never know for certain how others are going to react to words.

For instance, the word "alert" drives me crazy when anyone uses it. I know that's not fair and I know it's a very personal, maybe even unique reaction. The problem started with my mother (don't they all, the Freudians would ask?) My mother is always "alerting" me to things. She is very well-intentioned, but I would prefer if she alerted me that a meteor was heading straight for my house rather than alerting me that the price of tomatoes was going up. *Hey Mom, Newsflash—I don't cook and I don't care.*

I also have a particular dislike of the expression "serious money." You know, as in " For your serious money, let's invest in… " It's all serious to me. I could be arrested for assault and battery of a candy machine when it eats my 75 cents.

Then there's my son, who tells me that we go to Great Adventure for the same thing—to "have a great time." For him that means going 100 mph on the vomitron ride, and for me it means eating cotton candy and riding the carousel. Same objective? The words seem to say so.

Here's another far less personal example that some of you might find easier to relate to. Financial consultants often ask people what their goals and objectives are and write "retirement" when the client say "retirement." But "retirement" is just a word, it doesn't tell you whether it represents the best day of their life, or the worst. Are they retiring to something pleasurable or away from something painful? My friend George takes the same train to work each day. Whenever I see him at the station he greets me with a number. 1045. 1029. 987. He's counting down to his retirement. My father is eighty-five years old and goes to work every day because he wants to. He loves it. Retirement for him would be painful, not joyful.

When I was writing this book I became acutely aware of the different words I could use to describe my subject matter. For instance, I came up with audience, listener, and conversation-mate when I was trying to come up with a name for the person to whom I am speaking. Each of these words means something different to me, but I don't know if that is true for my reader. The word *audience* makes me think of more than one person, and it also makes me think of a performance of some sort. The performance part made me uncomfortable. The word *listener*, on the other hand, makes me think more in the lines of a conversation, but only one part of it, as if a listener is not also a speaker. And then there's *conversation-mate*, which I came up with because I couldn't think of an existing term that said it all for me. But conversation-mate doesn't actually say anything about listening. You may agree or disagree with my interpretations of these words this is a perfect example of how language can be limiting and even misleading.

Choose Your Words/Weapons Carefully

Be very careful when choosing your words, especially when discussing a sensitive subject or speaking to a person whom you know is sensitive. The less well you know your listener the more cautious you should be because you do not know what words are triggers for their emotions. Nor do you know what words have different meanings for them than for you. The best you can do is to look to the listener often for cues of understanding or miscommunication, and clarify what you mean whenever you have any doubt about how you are being received.

This is particularly the case with cross cultural communication. Some of my favorite examples are translations of phrases found outside of the United States:

- A dry cleaner in Hong Kong has a sign that says, "Drop your drawers here for best results."
- A hotel in Belgium has a sign that reads, "Our chambermaids will service you any way you want."

17

- A hotel in Paris has a sign that says, "Please leave your values at the front desk."
- A foreign airline has a sign that says, "We send your bags all over the world."
- The Scandinavian vacuum manufacturer, Electrolux, first used the following in an American campaign: "Nothing sucks like Electrolux." Now there's some copy I wish I wrote.
- When the dairy association expanded their marketing campaign "Got Milk?" to Mexico, in Spanish it translated to "Are you lactating?"
- Frank Perdue's chicken slogan "It takes a strong man to make a tender chicken" was translated into Spanish as "It takes an aroused man to make a chicken affectionate."

Because it takes a lot of energy to attempt to evaluate the conversational style, thinking style, and potential triggers of each person you speak to, I suggest that instead of focusing on the other person you focus first on yourself. Uncovering what makes someone else do what they do is never as important as deepening your own self-awareness. The following is my personal list of the things you can do right now to improve your verbal communication skills.

• Know what you want to say

If you aren't clear about what you intend to say *you won't know if and when you are being misunderstood*. If you have the time, try to rehearse what it is you want your listener to hear. Say the words out loud to yourself. Listen carefully to the words you plan to use and ask yourself if they are appropriate for your audience and if they accurately describe your intention. The messages of many speakers are often not heard simply because they were never transmitted.

• Get comfortable with not saying anything

The pause is not a cultural favorite in the West. Some people feel so uncomfortable during moments of silence that they'll say anything just to fill that space. If you are one of those people, I suggest you train yourself to incorporate pauses into your conversation. Think of it this way: Even if it is excruciatingly difficult to refrain from saying something, embracing the pause is always better than speaking without having thought about all of the implications of what you want to say.

Try this exercise: When you finish a sentence or when you are about to respond to someone, wait a couple of seconds before beginning. Count to four. Slowly. This demonstrates that you are spending a moment to make certain you are appropriately considering what is being said. Perhaps the reality is that you are terrified and you feel like you cannot possibly spend another nanosecond waiting for someone to say something. If that is the case, no one has to know. Just count to four.

What typically happens is that after you have *forced* yourself to pause a dozen times, you will begin to instinctively do it. And a bit after that, you will find that you begin to use those moments to *actually consider* your thoughts as well as those you have just heard. But if it hasn't been your nature until now to pause, it might be difficult to get the hang of it at first. I assure you that after you have attended to the cultivation of the pause for a week, you'll wonder how you survived without it for so long. You will discover that you have become a better speaker and a better listener.

Remember Jack Benny? On his radio show a robber accosted him and asked, "Your money or your life?" Benny paused. The robber repeated his question in a more agitated voice: *"Your money or your life?"* Benny paused again. Total silence. "I'm thinking, I'm thinking," he finally responded. The pause made the joke.

Jerry Seinfeld says a long pause after asking, "Can you do me a favor" indicates the favor is a really big one. Meanwhile, a short pause is indicative that the favor following the question is no big deal.

If you really want to learn about the impact of the pause, listen to tapes of Ronald Reagan, The Great Communicator. The man used pauses better than anyone I have ever seen. Whether for emphasis or to regroup, his pauses spoke volumes and pulled us in to hear his message.

• Choose words that are appropriate for your audience

This is largely a listening issue and will be discussed at length in Chapter Four. For now, understand that it is much easier to have a conversation with someone who likes you, and people tend to like people *who are like them*. Therefore, the more you tailor your word choice to the words of your listener, the more you appear to be like them, and the stronger affinity they will have for you. Appropriate word choice also makes conversations more efficient because it cuts down on the potential for misunderstandings and the need for clarification. Don't forget that you can easily lose any audience with language that is offensive, too technical, dull, boring, or repetitive.

Every profession is loaded with its own jargon. The rule of complete communication here, is to talk at the level of your audience. Do not talk at your own level of expertise if it is above theirs. And if you want them to understand some jargon that is not familiar to them, enlist the aid of my two favorite helpers, analogies and stories. When you use *analogies* and *stories*, you take the subject matter and the listener from the unknown to the known.

For example, in the financial services industry, the term *asset allocation* is a fancy way of saying: Don't put all of your eggs in one

19

basket. The way you would describe asset allocation would depend on whom you were speaking to. You might say:

- Asset allocation is like balancing your diet.
- Asset allocation is like taking vitamins to supplement the areas in which you aren't getting the proper nutrition.
- Asset allocation is like working out with weights to strengthen the areas of your body that are not as strong as you would like them to be.
- Asset allocation is like preparing for the future instead of trying to predict it.

The only rule for analogies is that in order for them to be most effective they should be appropriate for the audience.

As for stories, the only mistake you can make is to not make one up if you have to. When someone is not grasping what you have to say (or to avoid that situation altogether), a good hypothetical won't hurt anyone. Sometimes, all you have to do to get someone to see their situation in a more objective, or a more clear way, is to make up a story about them. Simply begin your story with, "I have this friend, I'll call him Sam, and he happens to have experienced something remarkably like what you are going through. Here's what happened..." After such an introduction, most people manage to be able to step outside of themselves for a moment in order to contemplate Sam's situation even though they know perfectly well that there is no Sam.

- **Leave room for dialogue**

Whether you are presenting to a group of 100 or speaking to your spouse, don't tell everything you know. Leave room for dialogue; engage your listener(s) in conversation. Usually, the person who thinks he is the smartest is the person who makes sure he does most of the talking. This is no secret, so if you don't want to come across as a know-it-all, let your audience know their thoughts are valued. Ask for their thoughts and make sure you thank them for their input every time.

- **Use what you know**

People respond in very predictable patterns. Therefore, if you know certain characteristics of a person you can easily predict how they will react and you should use that information accordingly. Pay attention to what people say and how they say it. For instance, if you are speaking with someone who always disagrees with you, anticipate that and say, "I know you're not going to like this...."

Others are constantly giving you rules for how they communicate—you show respect for them if you use those rules. Here are some other examples....

- Some people need to be in control and are terrified of every- thing falling apart. Two words to never use with such people are "don't worry," because they are natural pessimists and will become defensive. They'll say, "What do you mean don't worry, of course I'll worry, it's my God-given right." Worry fuels them and when you say "Forgeddaboudit," you create more anxiety for them. I worked with someone who had a great need to con- trol things. He came late to a meeting once, and he was the boss so it was okay. He made a beeline for the thermostat and turned it off, at which time someone said, "Willy, what are you doing?" His reply? "Reminding all of you that I control every- thing."
- Then there are pessimists. If you know someone is a pes- simist, the last thing you want to do is to assure them that everything will be great; all you'll get is a list of all of the things that can go wrong. The good thing about pessimists is that you can be sure that they are prepared for the worst. If you are ever on a small airplane and you hear a noise, hope there is a pessimist on board. I promise you the pessimist is ready for anything and everything to go wrong and has a parachute big enough to hold up the airplane—just in case.

- **Avoid extreme and definitive words**

Why? Because most extreme and/or definitive words are exagger- ations, hence they are dishonest communication. There are very few situations where *always* and *never* really fit; that is where they are *accurate* and *true*. There are plenty of books about the current power words and words you should avoid if you can. Though power words are trendy and change every year, most lists of words to avoid include definitive words such as: never, always, impossible, and can't, and the overuse and misuse of the words love and hate. Nobody *loves* broccoli.

- **Be careful with the word "but"**

Remember the Schoolhouse Rock song called "Conjunction Junction?" Conjunctions, the theme song told us, hook up words, phrases, and clauses. Though I am not about to argue with that, there is one particular conjunction that has a more complex effect than the mere hook-up. I refer, of course, to the word "but." Every time I hear it said, my mind automatically forgets whatever came before it, and amplifies the negative phrase that follows it. I am that conditioned. And most people are not far behind.

I understand that "but" is, theoretically, supposed to hook-up, to *connect*, what is before and after it. However, it doesn't always func- tion that way in reality. Instead, it tends to create a competition between the before and the after, and indicates that the winner was the after.

• Eliminate "to tell you the truth"

Another conversational culprit that it might be a good idea to eliminate is anything that makes you sound like you don't ordinarily tell the truth. Phrases such as "to tell you the truth," "frankly," or "to be perfectly honest with you," make you sound like you are breaking your usual habit of prevarication for a special occasion. They also imply that the listener should somehow be grateful that they are worthy of the truth.

Consider this: I wanted a change in my life, so, as women do, I got a haircut. I ask my husband, "What do you think of my new haircut?" He gleefully responds, "I love it—the style is fabulous, it really brings out your eyes, and it makes you look really thin, but, to be honest with you, I do think the bangs are a bit short." What do I hear? "Blah, blah, blah, blah, BUT ALL OF THAT IS A LIE BECAUSE THE BANGS MAKE YOU LOOK RIDICULOUS. FURTHERMORE, CONSIDER YOURSELF LUCKY THAT I DECIDED NOT TO LIE TO YOU!"

• Be careful with "try" and "hope"

Try and hope are two little words that create a disproportionate amount of stress. Experiments were done in a rehabilitation center at the University of Pennsylvania and the subjects were people who had strokes and were regaining their muscle strength. They were hooked up to electrodes and after the command, "Okay, now try harder," their strength decreased. Think about it. How confident do you feel if I tell you I will *try* to meet you on time tomorrow, or that I *hope* to be able to find the missing item you asked me to look for. Substitute "intend" or "anticipate" for "hope" and "try;" they engender far more confidence. This is hard to do.

• Be careful when being funny

The most wonderful thing about humor is the same thing that can make it a vicious weapon; it works best when it hits close to home. Therefore, my advice to everyone who incorporates *what they think is funny* into any conversation or presentation, is *know your audience*. And this advice is two-pronged. Knowing what the listener thinks is funny is very important, but knowing whether or not they will think it is funny coming out of *your* mouth is another story. Furthermore, just because something is funny, and you know your audience would think it's funny, *doesn't mean it needs to be said at the moment you think of it*. Timing, after all, is what makes great comedians great.

22

- **Be careful with off-color language**

Cussing, and other, less-blatant forms of off-color language, is always risky in front of groups of people whom you don't know. There's nothin' like cussin' to make you feel better sometimes; just be aware of who is within hearing distance. There are some impenetrable walls that go up when someone judges the language you are using as inappropriate. In their eyes, you may never recover from one off-color joke or remark. My advice is to always err on the side of caution.

- **Don't tell someone *not* to feel something they are telling you they are feeling**

The reality or intensity of someone else's feelings is not for you to judge. If you do not think a person's reaction is appropriate, discuss what you *think* about their reaction. Telling someone they are wrong for being angry or sad will get you nowhere. The same is true for telling them to cheer up. However, if you try to draw out the person's *thoughts* about their situation, you have a better chance at having a peaceful conversation because they will not feel accused of being dramatic. This also helps them separate their thoughts from their feelings, so you can clarify them for both of you.

Also, I have a particular aversion to the phrase "it's not that bad." No one is inside my head or heart or has felt what I have felt and even knows whether it is really that bad (whatever it is). And no one has *the right* to judge whether my emotion is over-the-top. Anything that sounds like you are invalidating someone's feelings is not a productive direction for your conversation. One of my favorite quotes is: "A [person's] emotional reaction seems inappropriate only as long as you can't see his or her memory" (Nichols, 91).

- **Don't fight fire with fire**

Whenever you are having a sensitive or hostile conversation and the other person becomes angry and starts to call you names or raise their voice, do not mirror their behavior, for it will only fuel them. In any conversation where there is disagreement or the objectives of the parties are at odds, resistance is a natural part of the exchange. Resistance can come in many forms, from a simply stated objection to outright animosity. Whenever you encounter behavior that is antagonistic, I suggest refraining from "giving it back." Trying to match or beat the other person tells them that you are agreeing to have an argument *because you are participating in the same way*. When you counter a sarcastic remark with your best banter, you have just mirrored that person and told them that you are just like them. Now, is that really your objective in such a situation?

So what do you do when someone becomes unreasonable? Ask them to *tell you more* about why they feel the way they do. Again, the real objective is to separate—and get the other person to separate—thoughts from feelings. Because feelings are fact when we are feeling them, telling someone not to feel what they are feeling is futile. And telling them that they are wrong for having their feelings or that the feelings themselves are wrong is worse.

Besides, when someone says something that you think is out of line—whether it is defensive or offensive—they are probably reacting from their emotions. Consequently, their emotions are likely to trigger an emotional response *in you.* At that moment, you have signed up for an argument that probably has nothing to do with what is really going on.

I'm sure you've heard the expression "hold your tongue". Next time, when someone verbally attacks you, *hold your emotions*, and use your *tongue* to diffuse the emotions and clarify the situation. Remember the old saying, "The tongue has no bones but it can break one's back." Use your tongue to request further explanation of the speaker's thoughts and feelings, and you'll transform a potential argument into a productive conversation.

The three words "tell me about…" open up any potentially closed conversation. If you ask a yes or no question, most people will give you a yes or a no answer without elaboration. If I ask my son, "Did you have a good time at the baseball game?" What do I get? "Yeah, mom." End of conversation. But if I say, "Tell me about the ball game"—I have given him a topic for at least a sentence or two, and by some standards that is actually a conversation.

• Get used to saying "I don't know"

As they say: "Sometimes we know more than we tell and sometimes we tell more than we know." I am a highly educated woman with a lot of life experience. Yet, until recently, when I didn't know the answer to something, even if there was no good reason why I should, I cringed (internally at least) every time I had to admit my ignorance. Not anymore.

I decided to let go of the hope that I could actually know everything there is to know. Sounds ridiculous? Well, what's more ridiculous: thinking you should know everything, or thinking that *anyone else thinks that you do know everything and will be shocked and dismayed to discover otherwise!* Saying "I don't know," "I don't understand," and "Would you please explain that to me?" lets people know you are human and are confident enough in what you *do* know to admit that there are things you *don't* know.

If you are giving a presentation and you are asked a question you don't know the answer to, acknowledge how great the question is and how important it is, and take responsibility for finding the answer, both for yourself and the other person. And don't forget to

24

call them with the answer; it'll come as a surprise and they will remember your effort, follow-through, and attention to detail.

- **"You think that's bad, well you should hear what happened to me ..."**

We all have a tendency to prescribe, usually out of our personal experience. When someone else tells a personal story, we immediately are reminded of an autobiographical tale that is similar. We are usually trying to offer advice based on our experience that is similar. There is nothing wrong with that unless you have a habit of telling your tale either during the other person's (which functions to completely invalidate whatever their thoughts were) or directly after, preceded by the words, "You think that's bad, well ... " (which makes you look like you are trying to compete with what they are saying). The idea is not to put the spotlight on yourself, but to communicate that because of your experience you truly understand. You *empathize*.

When someone is telling you about his experience, many times he is looking simply for acknowledgment that he is are being heard. One of the most powerful techniques of communications is to agree with the person you are listening to. The two words, "I understand" work miracles, especially if someone is in pain. Those words let them know that you acknowledge what they have expressed and they feel permitted to relax. When you meet the human need to be understood, you also meet the need to be appreciated and validated. The ears and hearts then open. Often being a good listener means just being a witness.

- **Articulate your standards**

Sometimes people have to be told what is acceptable and unacceptable, particularly in male-female relationships where communication is riddled with emotion, assumptions, and expectations. How many times have you taken someone's offensive behavior personally only to realize that they treat everyone that way? And how many times have you gotten angry with someone for doing something they always do (so why are you forever equally surprised by this predictable pattern?). The irksome behavior makes you angry every time, yet you never say anything. How many times have you become enraged with someone *for being who they are*.

In order to articulate your standards, you must first know what they are. What is offensive language to you and just how much of it can you take? What about jokes? Are there any topics that are off-limits? For me, I hate jokes that in any way make fun of people who are disabled. I spent several years in a rehabilitation facility watching in awe as courageous people tried to regain the use of their muscles.

25

Their dignity is not something to be mocked and I always discourage *and never laugh at* jokes that are at the expense of these people.

There will always be jokes, but you can do something to try to decrease their frequency in your presence and perhaps even in your absence. Remember that you cannot expect anyone to *not* cross any of your lines until they know where the lines are. Only you can establish them. And only when you discuss the unacceptable behavior of others (without attacking them personally) will you be able to better understand their motives and increase your intimacy and rapport. Eliminating people from your life because they do things that you find unacceptable is not as productive as trying to discover why they behave the way they do, trying to empathize, and then setting boundaries that allow you to continue with the relationship.

People I know do not tell jokes about disabled people because I have let them know that I find them offensive and thoroughly unacceptable. And because I did not attack them in the process, I wouldn't be surprised if they have curbed their joke telling of that nature more than I am aware. However, there are always people whose ways of being revolve largely around being offensive just for the sake of it. Expecting them to be anyone other than who they are, is setting yourself up for disappointment.

Another kind of joking is the mocking of a person in your presence. In Gordon MacKenzie's beautiful, charming book *Orbiting the Giant Hairball: A Corporate Fool's Guide to Surviving With Grace*, he recounts the confessions of a lifelong teaser. When I meet chronic teasers, I usually try to limit my interaction with them and I don't allow them to show me any other behaviors (I assume they are all just as bad). This quote from MacKenzie's book changed my mind.

> Far back as I could remember, I had always been a frenzied teaser but had never looked at why. Now I knew. I teased to control. Why would I want to control? Because I am afraid. For whatever reason, I have had a long-standing fear of others. One way of dealing with this fear was to learn the skill of teasing. I learned it well, eventually walling myself off with a bristling armor of barbed banter designed to blunt the power of those countless people I felt threatened by. My teasing became a weapon intended to push others off balance and thus reduce the sense of menace in my life (121).

An important distinction needs to be made about articulating your standards. You are doing it *for you*—not with the intention of trying to change anyone else. Setting out to change another person is sure to end in disappointment and resentment—at best. Besides, isn't it a bit arrogant to assume that you know how someone else should be behaving? As long as you have things you need to work on, why distract yourself from your own path of evolution to stop and judge someone else? Transform yourself to the best you can be, which includes letting people know when their behavior is unacceptable to you. Perhaps others will learn from your example. And if they don't, you should have no resentment because you haven't "wasted" your time trying to help (read: change) them (does that sound familiar?).

• Location, Location, Location

Have you ever had the frustrating experience of having the same conversation several times and it never goes the way you want it to (yet you persist)? In fact, you dread trying to have it because it always begins, proceeds, and ends the same way. If you have a particular topic that always ends with a stalemate, I suggest an actual *physical reframing*. Have the conversation in a place you've never had it before. Recall the way you are usually positioned, physically, when you have the conversation, and do something else. Escape the history of the conversation and create an alternate reality where a different outcome is possible. In the legal world, this is known as "change of venue," and it is necessary when there has been so much media coverage of a case that everyone in the area has made up their mind about how they feel. Choosing an unbiased jury and having a fair trial are unlikely, so the proceedings are moved to a different location.

A good place to discuss sensitive topics is when you are going on a long car ride. It is more private than an airplane and you have a captive audience. Be careful with "Your place or mine," because both places have oodles of potential triggers due the personal nature of the environment and whose "territory" it is perceived to be. Sensitive topics deserve the attempt to make both people comfortable and not on the defensive.

Furthermore, I suggest framing the communication as a process rather than a one-time transaction. This way, you allow for the possibility of thinking things over. For example, "Why don't we discuss this on Tuesday at home and then go over it again Friday evening at dinner?" Or, "Let's meet from 1 P.M. to 2 P.M. in your office on Thursday, take the weekend to jot down any thoughts we have, and review where we stand on Monday?"

• Learn how to deal with resistance

Why do people object? Because of psychological or logical resistance. Psychological resistance can include: preference for established habits, apathy, reluctance to give something up, unpleasant associations with the other person, the tendency to resist domination, predetermined ideas, or the fundamental dislike of making decisions. Some resistance is simply preoccupation. "All audiences—of one or 1,000—are preoccupied. They are thinking about their own problems, or what they are going to have for dinner, or how they can meet next month's bills. It's your job to break through this wall of preoccupation and get them to listen to you" (Berkley, 57). This is not personal, so don't take it that way.

Another form of resistance that has nothing to do with you (so you can't do anything about it), is *selective attention* and its counterpart, *selective recall*. The basic idea is that most people pay attention to those things they are familiar with, and then they recall them faster. And when they are attended to and recalled, it's as if they are more important than everything else that was happening at the time. Because you probably cannot know anyone so well that you are aware of everything that is important to them, by degrees, the most you can do is make what you say memorable, and I'll discuss that later.

Finally, the form of resistance that every person in sales is thinking about at this moment, is the objection. Understand that when someone voices an objection, they are trying to tell you something that is probably useful to you. Your first step is to assess whether the objection is sincere. In other words, people do not always tell you the real reason they are resisting. If they tell you something other than the truth and you solve the problem, you haven't gotten anywhere. For instance:

Q: Would you like to come over for coffee on Monday morning?
A: Thanks, but I have to wait for the plumber on Monday morning.
Q: Great, then I'll come to your house for coffee, okay?
A: Oh no, not that, my house is a mess ...
My answer? Perhaps they don't want to see you.

This can take many forms. Another example: You go to the coat store and the salesperson shows you a cashmere coat that is "so you" and you say the price is too high. The salesperson lowers the price, because it is going on sale in three days. Suddenly you don't like the color. The salesperson checks (with the manager, of course), and says, yes, you can get the cashmere coat in pink, and you can have it in a week. Remarkably, you realize you don't like the size of the collar. What you really want is a fur, but that's not politically correct. Meanwhile, the salesperson has wasted time because of their inability to get to the real issue—you don't want a cashmere coat—want a mink. They don't carry fur.

One very important question to ask when you are faced with resistance is "Am I on the right side of the problem?" The two sides to any objection are *the concept* and *the brand*. I ask my cousin if he wants to see the shoot-em-up movie (*brand*), and he says: "No, I don't like Clint Eastwood." So I suggest the girly-psychobabble movie (*brand*) and he responds: "You know I can't stand that stuff." I resort to inquiring about the newest animated feature film (*brand*), and he gives me that look that screams: "I have a two year old, remember? I get more than my fair share of cartoons!" At this point I have two choices: I could persist (recommending some more *brands*), or I could realize that he doesn't want to go to the movies (ah! my *concept* was off).

Net message? When someone is not sold on the concept side (the idea of a movie—or the idea of a cashmere coat from the prior example), you are in for a string of brand objections. The simplest way out of such a situation, is to ask: "Do you want to see a movie tonight?" (If yes), "Would you prefer to rent one or go to one?" This is a double concept sale. Once you have your answers, you can move to the brand side.

One technique for handling objections is to just let the other person dump their grievances on you as you listen carefully. Don't interrupt, as that will impair their listening because they will be preoccupied with their unstated objections. When they are finished, reiterate their points to assure them that you have listened and not judged. You might even want to number the points, as the enumeration is validating and adds a structure to your response.

Remember that when voicing objections, most people tend to be nervous and their anxiety might adversely affect the way they present their ideas. Be sympathetic and don't forget to thank the person for raising such helpful points. (Objections are, after all, helpful to you because they save you the time you might otherwise spend trying to unearth them). If they misspoke or weren't as articulate as they usually are, don't take this opportunity to correct or mock them. Instead, address as many of the objections as you can.

The other side of this technique is to raise the objections you believe they might have yourself, before they do so in a more aggressive way. This functions to minimize the impact of the objections *and* increase trust because you are bringing up points that aren't necessarily advantageous to you.

> For example, I say to my husband: "I think we should rent a house in the Hamptons this year. We always have such a good time, we know a lot of people out there, and there's a house available in our favorite town. I know you don't like the drive out there and I researched the jitney. I also talked to my boss about taking Fridays off so we can beat the traffic. What do you think?

Addressing objections before your listener lets the listener know that you are giving full thought-time to the issue because you have considered aspects that could be unfavorable to them. The listener is likely to feel more confident and trusting of you because you are presenting all of the facts. They don't have to search for holes because you are explaining the holes to them in advance. Furthermore, when you mention objections you are not on the defensive and the discussion has less of a probability of turning into a debate.

No matter how you choose to handle this type of situation, there is one type of response that will almost always get you into trouble: *Do not answer an emotional question with a logical answer.* If the person is reacting on an emotional level, first you have to take the sting out of what they are upset about or they won't even hear you. Rephrase what they said in a neutral way. If someone says to you: "I hate your guts and I never want to see you darken my door again," as much as you would like to retort, "That is hardly a mature response; let me know when you are ready to have a rational conversation," there is a better reply. Simply say, "I guess what you are telling me is that I have made you furious." I do not guarantee results with this technique, but if you add "and for that, I apologize," you have a great chance of avoiding a sparring match. You can only begin to fix the real problem after you have addressed the person's emotional state and given them a chance to vent.

The most common situation where the separation of emotions and logic is necessary is in communication between men and women. Perhaps this scenario sounds familiar ...

Example: Husband comes home late from work.

Wife, visibly upset, says: "Why were you late?

Husband says: "I was working." He then proceeds to the refrigerator to get a beer and then to the den, where he scrambles for a moment for the remote and then turns the television on. At no point does he look Wife in the eye.

Meanwhile, Wife, quite perturbed, follows him into the den. She observes what she interprets as a frantic search for the remote, and then she storms out of the room without saying a word. She is certain that he is keeping something from her, and that something is bad. Furthermore, that something is definitely related to his tardiness. If that were not the case, she assumes, he would have looked her in the eye, given her a hug, and told her how much he missed her while he was working late. Or at least he *should* have.

Husband and Wife are now officially in a fight, at least according to Wife.

How did this happen? Because Husband does not realize that "Why were you late?" really meant "You didn't call—why didn't you call—who were you with—was it really your job—is your job more important than me—I was worried about you—why didn't you call to let me know that you were going to be late—don't you care about me at all?"

Essentially, Wife's question was really a request for reassurance that Husband cares. The moment he saw that Wife was upset, he should have immediately realized that giving her any kind of straight, logical answer, was not going to work. Why? Because Wife's real need at the moment was for reassurance—not an answer to her question.

As soon as you notice that the person you are with is acting and speaking from their emotions, the best technique for avoiding an argument or misunderstanding is to ask yourself the following questions:

- What did the person say? And I mean literally. What were their actual words?
- What could they have meant by those words? (Take the clue from their emotional state)
- What is the real need at the moment? (Probably unrelated to the words)
- Address the real need.
- Proceed to address the question, if it even matters any longer.

Separating the emotional from the literal takes a bit of finesse and humility; some people find it difficult to bypass an opportunity to mock someone who is acting from their emotions. But if you want to maintain peace, fix the person first, and if a problem still exists, try to fix that next.

Persuasion

I contemplated not including a discussion about persuasion because I was feeling that it denoted manipulation to some people. But persuasion doesn't have to mean manipulation. Manipulation is trying to get someone to do something they do not want to do. It is very much a mind game where you try to back the other person into a corner where their only response is "I'll take it," regardless of whether or not they really want it. Persuasion, on the other hand, is an appeal to the head and the heart. It is about uncovering what someone really wants and then showing them how you can help them get it.

You can make a great impact when you touch someone's emotions—when you make them feel warmth, empathy, and involvement in what you are talking about. People become involved in what you are talking about when they become involved with *you*. If you are likeable and compassionate, and what you say is interesting and memorable, you are in the best position for them to truly trust and understand you. Persuasion is just a natural, effortless by-product of that trust.

There are three steps of effective persuasion.
1. Know what you really want.
2. Find out what the other person really wants.
3. Develop rapport and speak and listen with intent so that both of you get what you really want (win/win).

When you know what your intentions are and you express them in a way that is appealing to your listener, you accomplish two things: you built trust and you build rapport. People tend to not trust you if they don't know why you are talking to them. Their mind instantly wanders to all of the ways you could be trying to manipulate them and all of the things you could be trying to sell them. Once they know what you want, they feel comfortable with you. And the more you phrase your intentions in a way that mirrors the way that they speak and behave, the greater the affinity they will have for you.

Being honest about your intentions is a win/win behavior. The win/win situation is one where both parties get what they want—not where both give up something to get something (that would be a lose/lose, don't you think?). It is not about compromise; it is about helping someone meet their needs while meeting your own. The error is in assuming that your needs are necessarily in opposition. Your job is to let them know that you know what they need and you can help them get it.

The above steps of effective persuasion are based on the premise of cooperation rather than competition. The simplest way to produce a win/win situation is to create an environment where all parties will feel good about the outcome and benefit from it. This involves educating them about how you arrived at your viewpoint, re-capping what you believe their viewpoint to be, and all of the plusses and minuses of what you would like to happen. This kind of explanation is not adversarial. In fact, you are both on the same side. This kind of presentation promotes trust and leads to a win/win.

When you build trust and rapport, the other person will gladly tell you how they really feel and what they really want. Learning how to communicate effectively and empathetically means listening and facilitating this process so you establish how they think and feel.

In *The Seven Habits of Highly Effective People*, Steven Covey advises, "Seek first to understand, then to be understood." Once you know where the other person is coming from, and you have let them know in your own words, they feel understood. They also feel appreciative that you have taken the time and energy to clarify and validate their position. And once you understand them, *and they are convinced that you understand them*, it is easier to present them with information in a way that they will be receptive to.

One of the most effective ways to build trust and rapport, is to leave people feeling BLUE:

B is for Believability. The old adage is true: People don't care how much you know until they know how much you care. They need to feel your confidence, your conviction. They need to see it in your face and your mannerisms, and hear it in your voice.

How confident would you feel if you went to a doctor who looked at your x-rays and said, "Hmmmm. Hmmmm. Well, I don't know, it could be a blockage or it could be a hot dog. What did you eat for lunch?"

L is for likeability. If you demonstrate empathy and show understanding, people will like you. My dear friend, Angie Clark, one of the best and most successful salespeople on Wall Street, has a couple of favorite, all-purpose responses. One is "I understand." These words reassure and comfort. They let the speaker know that they are not being judged or dismissed. She also says, "You're right." This diffuses hostility and creates likeability. No one will then proceed to argue with themselves.

U is for Understand. If you want people to go along with your ideas and recommendations, they must understand you. Therefore, you must make yourself understood. No one buys anything when they are feeling dumb. Instead, they are more likely to nod and say "Let me think about it," or "I have to ask my spouse, do you have a brochure?" When we don't understand we tend to shut down and the conversation is over.

E is for Excited. The listener must be excited about what you have to say. Enthusiasm and negativity are both contagious. Whichever you sincerely project is the one that those around you will feel. It's even good for your health; new research says optimists live longer.

Further, even if you aren't feeling particularly positive, rather than getting caught in the trap of "I feel horrible, therefore my life must be horrible," change your relationship to whatever situation is bothering you—change your language—and your feelings with change. Hans Selye was a pioneer in the medical side of the relationship between the mind and body. Among other things, he helped us think of stress and negativity as the *perception* of an event, and *not* the event itself. Whatever event occurs cannot be altered in any way. However, your perception of that event, *your relationship to* that event, is something that is totally in your control. You are always free to change the way you think about and relate to a situation; the choice is yours. The latest findings in the field of psychoneuroimmunology, which studies the relationship between the mind and body, continue to provide evidence that our thoughts can—do—affect our health. When you choose to think positively, your body follows and reacts positively.

Finally, don't forget that the most powerful way to persuade anyone of anything, is to let them know how much and in what ways they will benefit from your idea/product. Most people want to know what's in it for them, and are more likely to listen, and go along with you, if they are getting something they desire. And the more they think they will get, the more interested they will be. The only caveat is to *not* assume you know what the other person wants.

For example: Jack and Jill are house hunting. The realtor shows them a beautiful old Victorian house, on a hill, overlooking a lake. The realtor lists the many features of the house, such as the spectacular view, the topnotch school system, the enormous kitchen and spacious den, and the very expensive, impeccably finished wood floors. Sounds irresistible? Not to Jack and Jill. Most of those features are just that— features—not benefits specific to Jack and Jill.

Jack and Jill *do* think the house is beautiful. But it is on the apex of a hill, in Maine, and getting up that hill in the snow and ice is probably no day the beach. And considering Jack and Jill aren't planning on having children, the feature of the topnotch school system is irrelevant. They are looking for a permanent home for the next twenty or thirty years, so the school system's quality isn't even a pertinent issue in the appraisal-value-at-resale discussion. Furthermore, Jill loves wool carpet and is planning on covering the floors with it, so the appeal of the wood floors is limited. On the upside, the size of the rooms is a plus.

What the realtor did was what we in sales call a "Feature Fling Against the Wall." The Feature Fling Against the Wall is when the salesperson really doesn't know what the customer wants, so she simply lists all of the features of the product/idea, and hopes that some of them stick to the wall. In the above example, only the room size-feature was a real benefit to Jack and Jill, and the other features slid right off the wall.

The rule regarding features is: When it comes to trying to sell someone on the features of something, *make sure those features are a benefit to the customer before you pitch them*. Do not present a feature as a benefit unless it is—to your customer.

Talking to Yourself

Just as there are guidelines for what to say to others, there are guidelines for your internal conversations. Are you kind to yourself, or do you mumble things like: "I'm such an idiot/loser/moron/ (insert the insult of your choice)." Your choice of words—when you are talking to yourself—is of vital importance because those words are essentially your thoughts. And the thoughts you have cause and control both your emotions and your actions. And they also affect your health. Therefore, if you change your language, you change your consciousness, and you change your behavior. When your consciousness changes, your behavior will change.

In their seminal book on Rational Emotive Behavioral Therapy (REBT), *A Guide to Rational Living*, authors Albert Ellis and Robert A. Harper discuss the idea that we create our feelings with our thoughts. Our disturbing emotions can actually be traced back to thoughts and what Ellis and Harper call Irrational Beliefs, which can be changed. When the thoughts are changed, the emotions follow. Our thoughts are constantly sending us messages about what to feel. "[A] large part of what we call *emotion* stems from a certain kind—a biased, prejudiced, and strongly evaluative kind—of thinking. What we usually label as *thinking* consists of a relatively calm appraisal of a situation, a cool-headed analysis of its elements, and a reasonable conclusion about it" (26).

Considering your words create your experiences, it is imperative that you are very careful with words and phrases such as can't, never, and impossible, in addition to the way you talk about yourself. Change your problems to challenges, your debacles into learning opportunities, and if you ever misspeak something negative, promptly cancel it (actually say "cancel" out loud after you have misspoken—I'm not kidding). Remember that if you project negative thoughts, you will attract negativity.

One of my favorite *Tongue Fu'isms* (from Sam Horn's *Tongue Fu: How to Deflect, Disarm, and Defuse Any Verbal Conflict*—more from Horn in the Humor section of Chapter Five) is: "The mind is literal and is unable to focus on the reverse of an idea" (55). I have heard this principle explained many times before, but Horn's is my favorite explication of this reality that many people find hard to believe.

> Please do not picture a tall fountain glass filled with a mouth-watering hot fudge sundae. Do not picture the mounds of delicious, melted chocolate rolling down the sides of the rich vanilla ice cream. Stop your mind from thinking about the stack of frothy white whipped cream topped with a bright red cherry. Don't imagine dipping your long spoon into that delectable combination of yummy flavors, bringing it up to your lips, tasting it with the tip of your tongue.

Can you *not* do it? Your mind focuses on the word pictures and doesn't heed the directives, *not, stop,* and *don't.*

This is why you should frame what you say in the positive when you speak, even if you are trying to avoid something (e.g., "I will not hit the tennis ball out of bounds" is better stated as "I will hit the tennis ball within the boundaries").

Think about the times you have tried, and been unsuccessful at, changing your reaction to something in your life. How many women have said to themselves, "I will not get upset when my husband comes home and plops himself down on the couch, grabs the remote, and doesn't seem to notice I exist." How many times does it work?

The most important aspect of verbal communication to embrace, whether you are talking to someone else or talking to yourself, is that each word you choose matters, and some can even alter your body chemistry and your health. Choose with care and intent, for your words have the power to change lives.

Self-Discovery Exercise #1: What You Say

As I noted in Chapter One, five of the chapters of this book address different aspects of communication. Part of becoming a Complete Communicator is determining the kinds of changes you need to make in order to improve the way you relate to others. Recall that I suggested using a five-subject notebook in which to write comments about where you are and what you need to do.

Now that you have read this chapter, it is time to put your notebook to use. Using your microcassette recorder, record random conversations you have this week. In addition, ask your trusted friend, your buddy, to pay particular attention to the actual words you use. You may even want to show your buddy this chapter so he has a better idea of what to look for.

When you first use the microcassette recorder, you might find that you are so aware of being recorded that you alter your speech in some way. That alone tells you something. Write down how you felt about recording yourself and the things you notice about your words. And when you play back your tapes, write your own assessment of your language. Finally, ask your buddy for his input.

This informal method of assessment/self-assessment will give you valuable insights into the kinds of things you need to improve. Try to concentrate on your actual words for this exercise, because the next aspect of communication you are going to tackle—how you say it—plays an important part in how your words actually come across.

Summary

- The words you use are reported to account for 7 percent of your message, so choosing them carefully is of utmost importance.
- Know what you want to say before you open your mouth
- Get comfortable with not saying anything
- Pay attention to your audience and choose words that are appropriate for them.
- Use analogies and stories to explain concepts that are unfamiliar or difficult to understand
- Ask others for input and allow them time to complete their thoughts
- Pay attention to the clues your listener is giving you about the way he or she wants to be spoken to/treated
- Avoid extreme and definitive words
- Be careful with the word "but"
- Eliminate "to tell you the truth"
- Be careful with "try" and "hope"
- Be careful when being (what you think of as) funny
- Limit off-color language
- Don't tell someone *not* to feel something they are telling you they are feeling
- Don't fight hostility with more hostility
- Get used to saying "I don't know"
- Don't play "can you top this..." in conversation
- Let people know what you think is acceptable/unacceptable in conversation
- If a recurring conversation is difficult each time, take it to a new location to try to escape its history
- Learn how to deal with resistance by first determining the precise nature of the resistance
- Persuasion has three major elements
    - Know what you really want
    - Find out what the other person really wants
    - Develop rapport and communicate with intent so both of you get what you really want (win/win)
        - Rapport is developed by leaving by being believable, likeable, easy to understand, and exciting to listen to.

And finally,

- You can change your consciousness and your behavior by changing the way you talk *to yourself.*

CHAPTER THREE

How You Say It

One of my favorite books on speaking is *Speaking to Influence: How to Unlock the Hidden Power of Your Voice*, by Susan Berkley. She provides "voice mastery training" in her VoiceShaping®, workshops, and has some great tips that go beyond technique. I particularly resonate with the following:

> "Get in touch with the **essentials** of your message and the particulars of delivering it will be that much easier to master. The most powerful essential is love. Touch the heart of the listener and they'll barely notice if your voice is less than mellifluous or if your hand gestures are a little too choppy. In fact, many communication problems are caused because the speaker is temporarily out of touch with their essence. A monotonous speaker has lost touch with his essential enthusiasm. A dry, humorless speaker has temporarily lost touch with his essential joy. A theoretical speaker has lost touch with his humanity.... Vocal charisma, then, is what happens when heart meets technique (ii-iii).

Although I am going to give you tips that are technical in nature about how to be a better speaker, I agree with Berkley that all of the technique available to you will not help you as much as being in touch with your essence.

Self-Discovery Exercise #2: How You Sound

Before you do anything to change the way you speak, I suggest you *not assume that you know what needs to be changed.* It is well worth the small investment of time and money to purchase the micro-cassette recorder I have recommended. Your buddy can tell you what you sound like *to him*, which will inevitably involve interpretation from his perspective. However, when you tape your natural speech for a couple of days while you are out and about, and then you listen to how it really sounds, the resulting assessment could very well be different from your buddy's.

The microcassette recorder is especially useful here because our voices do not sound the same to us as they do to the world outside of our heads. Therefore, operating on the assumption that the way you sound equals what you hear *in your own head* means you are beginning your evaluation of your voice with a false premise. Unfortunately (according to most people), when you play back your recording of your voice, you are hearing it as those around you do. I have yet to meet a person who isn't appalled when they hear their voice for the first time. Many people think they sound nasal and whiny. And some do. But most people don't have too far to go to improve their voices.

I am a firm believer that a good, compassionate friend can save you a lot of money in consultant's bills trying to determine what needs to be improved in your speaking style. If, in addition to your microcassette recorder, you ask your buddy to apprise you of any undesirable speaking habits you have, you will probably be able to eradicate your most frequent and obvious problems without the help of a professional. If possible, ask your buddy to write down comments and suggestions, as the appropriate time to give advice is not always the moment you think of it. Show your buddy this chapter so he has an idea of what to look out for.

In addition, sometimes it is helpful to practice your presentation or conversation in front of people who are not familiar with your topic. If what you are saying is unclear or ambiguous to them, or if you sound very angry or sarcastic to them, you need to work on your tone and/or wording. People who are completely unrelated to the situation you are practicing for will not have any preconceived notions of how you should *be*. This makes their reactions that much more useful to you.

After you have listened to a couple of days of your voice, write down your reaction and any comments or suggestions about what you need to improve in the second section of your five subject notebook. Do the same after a week of listening to your friend's thoughts about your voice. The data from one week will probably be more than sufficient to help you make progress toward a better voice.

Improving the Sound of Your Voice

We begin, once again, with the basics. What is it you want to accomplish and who is your audience the majority of the time? The starting point when contemplating how to approach your audience is their head and heart. They lead the dance. Therefore, whenever you have a choice to make during your conversation/presentation, step into the shoes of your audience and make your choice from there.

If your plan is ever to persuade someone to do something, you must first determine whether they agree or disagree with you— *whether they need to be persuaded*. And in order to do that, you must create an atmosphere where such things can occur. Your vocal atmosphere includes:

- How fast you speak (sometimes fast-paced speech is more appropriate than at other times).
- How high your voice is (does it seem too high or low and is there anything you can do about that without straining your voice?).
- Can you hear your breathing or swallowing?
- Do you have an accent that either prevents people from being able to understand you or might bias them against you in any way (ask someone from the Bronx or Minnesota how people reacted to them when they visited California)?
- Does your voice go up or down at what seems to be inappropriate moments?
- Do your inflections have a pattern (e.g., many people, particularly women, end their sentences as if they were asking a question—with an upward inflection)? Is your inflection different for emotional topics than it is for more informational ones?
- Is your tone of voice appropriate (e.g., any sentence that you can comfortably add "of course, you moron" to means your tone of voice could use some improvement)
- Do you freeze up in any situation and find yourself unable to speak?

Breathing

When I talk about presentation skills I get a lot of questions about the proper way to breathe when giving a presentation. Oddly enough, no one ever asks me for advice on how to breathe when they are talking to their spouse or a friend. If you do not have a breathing technique (i.e., you try to breathe a lot, you try to keep your breathing to a minimum, you try to breathe deeply, you try not to breathe too deeply) when you are talking to your best friend, why do you need one when you are addressing a roomful of strangers?

I think that the real problem here is being able to relax enough to not pay attention to your breathing, hence *creating the need for a breathing technique*. If you have a breathing problem that manifests only in certain situations, it is your relationship to those situations that must be examined. Once you change your relationship to those situations (which usually involves changing your perception of them and your thinking about them), breathing should cease to be an issue.

The breathing technique I use is from yoga. Try it. Breathe in deeply through your nose. Let the air fill your stomach (your stomach should distend fully). Hold this position, and your breath, for several seconds and then exhale fully through your mouth. This is really filling your lungs with air. Once you have breathed deeply a couple of times, let your breathing return to its normal pace and depth. Note what it feels like and what it sounds like. Now begin reading this page aloud and just read and breathe, read and breathe, using the punctuation as a guide (that's why it's there). Unless you are trying to elicit some kind of extreme emotion in your listener, this is what you should sound like. If you needed to take a breath, it should have been taken at the comma in the last sentence, or the period. It's as easy as that.

Volume

If you are speaking in front of a group, it is far better to speak louder than softer; it sends the message that you have conviction. If you have a choice, use a microphone. Either way, fill the room with the sound of your voice.

If you are having a one-on-one, assume the pace and the volume of the person to whom you are speaking. Nothing undermines credibility more than one person talking like a runaway locomotive, at the speed of sound, while the other is moving at the speed of molasses. Besides, when you speak at the same pace and volume as your listener, you are demonstrating that you are like them by assuming their characteristics. This increases your own likeability, because we like people who are like us.

Intensity and Tone

"The reason we don't recognize the impact of our tone of voice is that we hear what we feel like, not what we sound like" (Nichols, 100).

Your voice should vary in intensity and tone. You don't want your voice to be flat and monotone, the auditory version of the Great Plains; you want it to be more like the mountains of Colorado. Your voice should go down at the end of a statement because that conveys certainty. If you are uncertain, or are asking a question, your voice should go up.

Oddly, many people have developed the habit of making everything sound like a question. This is particularly prevalent among women and more so among young women. In some cases it is a regional, linguistic trend. In others, it is a manifestation of a lack of self-esteem, where the speaker always seems to be saying, "Is what I am saying really true?" The latter screams of a lack of confidence and the need for others' approval.

Another habit, which is more indicative of an overall attitude, is the propensity toward the sarcastic tone of voice. In some parts of the country, and I'm thinking particularly of New York, sarcasm is a way of life for some people. Banter is often a measure of how quick, intelligent, and creative you are. I once heard someone say: "In New York City, warning signs of psychosis are often mistaken as personality." Meanwhile, in most other parts of the country, sarcasm is thought of as just plain rude. As always, know your audience and tailor your voice to that audience if you want them to like you.

The fastest way to establish whether you need to attend to your tone of voice is to ask your mother. But because that could result in an argument, I suggest asking your buddy. If your mother and your buddy are unavailable, there is a simple exercise you can do yourself, and it involves the microcassette recorder. Relying on the recordings when you are assessing your own tone of voice is generally not a good idea, as you are likely to think you sound just fine. You probably think you sounded fine the first time all of that came out of your mouth. And if you do have a bad tone of voice, you are likely to justify it because you are focusing on why your tone of voice was bad rather than the simple reality that it was bad.

But with the addition of one, small step, the recording of your voice becomes far more valuable to you when trying to evaluate its tone. When you listen to a tape of your voice, simply ask yourself: If I were to add "you dummy," to the end of the sentence that just came out of my mouth, does it make perfect sense? If so, your tone of voice needs improvement. For example, say: "That's not the way I told you do to it." Does "you dummy" provide a fitting end, given the way you read the sentence? Explore the different ways of reading that sentence. With finesse and care, it doesn't have to sound condescending.

Emphasis

Read the following sentence aloud. *I didn't say he stole the money.* What does that sentence mean? Do you know for certain? Well that depends on how you read it; it has multiple meanings depending on which word you gave the greatest emphasis. Try reading the same sentence, this time emphasizing the underlined word.

I didn't say he stole the money.

I didn't say he stole the money.

I didn't say he stole the money.

I didn't say he stole the money.

I didn't say he <u>stole</u> the money.

I didn't say he stole <u>the money</u>.

This is a perfect example of how emphasizing different words creates different meanings for the sentence. When you listen to recordings of your voice, note how emphasis actually dictates what a word or phrase means.

Speech fright

Some people know what they want to say and practice what they want to say, yet their intended words never leave their mouth. Instead, their speech is full of "uhhhhhs," "ummms," and choppy, incoherent phrases that vaguely resemble what they intended to say. There is a psychological reason why this occurs, and that psychological reason causes a physical reaction.

The psychological reason is usually related to some kind of anxiety about the reason for the conversation, or the speaking itself (as in the case of giving presentations). The anxiety often originates in the desire to not make any mistakes or sound in any way foolish. Unfortunately, this is a habit that needs to be eliminated as soon as possible, because audiences can be relentlessly cruel and I guarantee you that some people will begin to count each "uhhhhh," and might even be rude enough to tally them up and let you know what your total is.

There are also physical symptoms that often develop when you are full of anxiety about a particular communication. When the anxiety commences, there is a corresponding, temporary flood of two hormones in the bloodstream. These hormones, adrenaline and noradrenaline, cause your breathing to become rapid and shallow, your heart to race, and your pupils to dilate. They also affect the secretion of saliva which may cause symptoms such as the need to swallow.

Managing speech fright is a matter of being aware of events that cause you anxiety, and then working on relaxing and breathing prior to those events. Deep breathing, such as in the yoga exercise I mentioned, will help to slow your heart rate and relax your muscles. Relaxation can also come from your inner speech. Telling yourself that you are relaxed and prepared to speak, and that your speech is fluid and your breathing is unencumbered, can actually create those physical realities.

The Optimal Sound for Your Voice

You can take courses on changing your accent and learning how to breathe more effectively (i.e., knowing the right moment to pause and to take a breath in preparation for a thought that you don't want to interrupt). But when you have chosen your words and you are clear about what your intent is, your tone, pitch, and intensity should be a natural extension. If you are *trying* to sound like something other than what you are thinking and feeling, some part of you will leak the truth to your audience. They won't necessarily be cognizant of what is occurring, but they will notice that there is something about you that is insincere. The optimal sound for your voice is the one that emanates naturally from you when you are calm, sincere, and clear about what you want your listener to hear. Whether the message that is sent is the message that is heard is the topic of the next chapter.

Summary

When you record yourself and ask your buddy to listen carefully to your voice, attend to:

- the pace of your speech
- the pitch of your voice
- the volume of your voice
- your breathing and swallowing
- your accent
- your inflections
- your tone
- your emphasis

The optimal sound for your voice is the one that emanates naturally from you when you are calm, sincere, and clear about what you want your listener to hear.

CHAPTER FOUR

How You Listen

"There are few rewards for listening—mainly punishments for not listening" (Burley-Allen, 37).

I have spoken to thousands of people about listening and what is most memorable about almost all of these discussions, is how confused most people are about what exactly listening is supposed to look like and what it is supposed to achieve. My response to this apparent confusion is that I am not surprised. Considering how much time we spend listening (or at least appearing to be listening), and how little formal education we get as to how to do it, it makes sense that most of us aren't clear about what it is and what it involves.

For instance, many people confuse listening with probing for information. Have you ever been accused of "grilling" or "interrogating" your child or spouse, when all you thought you were doing was trying to be a good listener? If you have, chances are you need some tutelage in listening. And it's no wonder! We are born with the ability to hear, but listening is a skill that must be acquired and mastered with intent.

I like to think of listening as the subtle art of maximizing hearing and attention. I call it a subtle art because it is not some kind of process with standard instructions, although I have seen such things. The 1990s brought a renewed interest in the teaching of listening, which was a welcomed trend considering how competent we are believed to be at it (a mere 25 percent effective). Listening skills have even become a prominent part of management training programs.

I can say with near certainty, that at no point in the formal education of the readers of this book were you required to take a course on listening in grammar school, high school, or college. So why is it that something that takes up so much of our time (the lowest estimate I have seen is 45 percent) is the same thing that is all but absent in our schools' curricula?

Most likely the answer is that we do not value silence as much as we do speech. Silence is not thought to be the hallmark of assertive, authoritative, powerful people. Somewhere along the line silence became synonymous with weakness. For instance, salespeople are trained to be concerned first with *what they say*. They know which words elicit the reactions they seek, and they spend a lot of time thinking about how to phrase their sentences to position themselves exactly where they want to be in the conversation. On day three of a three-day training course, when they've already mentally (if not physically) checked out, there might be a small section on listening. Meanwhile, though speaking is not always a good idea, listening in silence is rarely a mistake.

Obstructions to Listening

Why do we process certain messages or parts of messages and disregard others? Because of our interests, attitudes, beliefs, and values. The more of these things that are shared, the easier communication tends to be. I say easier because you have less explaining to do with someone who is "on your wavelength," meaning either they actually think in the same manner you do, or they share the same opinions.

However, I would argue that the most successful and effective communication takes place between people who do *not* share a wavelength. If two people become aware that they are not thinking the same way, then manage to understand each other and accurately express how they think and feel—*that's* successful communication.

There are some physical barriers to listening, in addition to the less palpable factors such as other people's ways of thinking or their history with certain issues or words. For instance, the pitch of someone's voice can be so irritating to you that you find it difficult to listen. Though you cannot do anything about that, you can make sure your voice doesn't prohibit others from listening (see Chapter Three).

In addition, behaviors that could easily distract you while you are trying to listen include:

- Tapping fingers, pen, foot
- General fidgeting
- Staring, either directly in your eyes, or elsewhere in order to avoid eye contact
- Tone of voice
- Frequent checking of the watch
- Being constantly interrupted

Listening and Your Emotions

"Most failures of understanding are not due to self-absorption or bad faith, but to defensive reactions that crowd out understanding and concern" (Nichols, 3).

Each of us has characteristic ways of reacting emotionally in key relationships. Often we don't hear what is said because something in the speaker's message triggers hurt, anger, or fear in us. Unfortunately, all the advice in the world about "active listening" can't overcome the maddening tendency to react to each other this way.

In order to maximize your potential as a listener, you need to reflect upon the words, tones, and situations that trigger your emotions. Becoming aware of what upsets you will help you recognize and perhaps alter the way you react. What triggers you often has nothing to do with the speaker, *whose message gets lost while you are busy reacting emotionally.* Improving your listening entails gaining control over anything that prevents you from really hearing the message of the speaker, or distorting the message with your cloud of emotions.

"Good communication means having the impact you meant to have, that its intent equals impact. But every message must pass first through the filter of the speaker's clarity of expression and second through the listener's ability to hear what was said. Unfortunately, there are many times when intent doesn't equal impact" (Nichols, 40).

Listening Defined

The purpose of listening is to understand in an empathic way. In order to truly understand another, you must give that person the chance to explain how they feel and what they think, without judging or mocking them. Or appeasing them. Just saying "yes" or "uh huh" and/or nodding your head while thinking of what you are going to say, does not constitute listening.

Your ability to hear the real message of the speaker depends in large part on your own state of mind when they are speaking. "The state one is in will filter or affect the final result of our interpretation and understanding of any experience we have at that moment" (Hogan 223). In other words, the degree to which the listener is receptive is as important as the message sent by the speaker when determining the outcome on an exchange. The listener is as responsible as the speaker.

"The way you listen to and respond to others will strongly influence how they will respond back to you and how they will feel about your response, such as wanting to continue talking, feeling turned off or understood, tense or relaxed" (Burley-Allen 106).

47

Many people act as if listening were a competitive exercise where the first one to draw a breath is the listener. Many are stuck on transmit, merely waiting for their chance to hit the other with all of the profundities they've been mentally working on while the other was speaking.

Once we feel we have enough information to categorize, we stop listening. Barbara Langer, in her book *Mindfulness*, calls us *cognitive misers* because of our propensity to jump to a conclusion as soon as we believe we have enough information to do so. I'd like to say we do this to conserve our precious cognitive energy, but I don't think that's the case. The real story is more like: we make a quick judgment and then are distracted by a word, which begins a chain of thinking totally unrelated to what is supposed to be important at that moment. The result is that we don't really give ourselves the opportunity to process the entire message correctly.

Here's an example. I am listening to a client talk about his financial goals: this is a conversation we have had many times, so I assume he is saying the same ole' stuff. He says, "My financial goals are..." He has just lost me. My mind goes something like: "Goals ...goalie ...my son's soccer game ...gotta find out how he did...have to call the coach to change his position ...and how 'bout that new position my brother got...better call him too". Meanwhile, my client could be saying something completely different this time, but I never give myself the opportunity to find out.

Speaking that Improves Listening

The quality of the listening in any communication situation is not the sole responsibility of the listener. The speaker and the listener are not adversaries, they are on the same side. There are things they both can do to optimize any conversation.

In order to increase the probability that your communication will be successful, as a speaker, your first order of business is to have a plan: to decide what it is you intend to communicate. Not having a plan is like going to the grocery store without knowing what you want to cook, it's random and it probably won't be as efficient. If there are several things you want to say, number your list and inform your audience of how many items are on it. Enumerating is a way of anchoring information and tying it to an expectation; it tells people how long they will be listening for.

Next, before opening your mouth, consider your audience. The better you know them, the more you'll know about which words or phrases you should use, and which ones you should probably avoid. If you do not know your audience, there are several guidelines that you can follow when communicating with anyone about just about anything.

- **Likeable**

In order to increase the odds that your audience will be receptive to you, that they will be in the best position to listen to you, you should be as appealing as possible to them. When we like someone we tend to listen to them. And we tend to like people who are *like us*. **Rapport** develops at the subconscious level when someone believes you are similar to them and you understand them. Feeling instantly at ease with someone, being on the same wavelength, having a powerful connection, is your objective. The next chapter will explain exactly what you need to do to become more likeable and increase rapport.

- **Memorable**

A useful tip for making yourself memorable as a speaker is to differentiate yourself from the crowd. I attended a lecture given by a man who began by saying: "Tonight, I want to talk to you about your PMS." Is he looking at me, I wondered? Then, in his squeaky, scratchy voice that was somewhere between Ross Perot and Yoda, he said, "Your physical, mental, and spiritual life." I remembered PMS because he made it easy. And I remembered *him* because he used PMS.

The invisibles of Chapter Six will give you tips on humor and creative thinking, both of which will help you make you more memorable as a speaker.

- **Meaningful**

Humans are self-centered creatures. We tend to use ourselves as a point of reference; we use ourselves as the standard when assessing new things. Think about it. I ask you how tall your friend James is and your thought process goes something like this: Well, I am 5'5", and he is definitely taller than me, so I'd say maybe he's 5'9".

Chances are, if a speaker is talking about something that is meaningful to you as an individual, you will remember it. Furthermore, you will want to hear more, and you will be paying close attention for more information that is somehow related to you.

When you are a speaker, you want your audience to feel that you have customized what you are saying to them. Naturally, this is more difficult with larger audiences, but that's no excuse not to try. The moment you find out you are to give a speech or presentation, find out as much as possible about your audience and tailor what you are saying to them. I am not just talking about using vocabulary that is at their level or from their industry, I am talking about meaning. This works very well with one person or a handful of people. However, it is more challenging as the numbers grow, and more important, as the *heterogeneity* of the group increases. In other words, a large group of similar people is easier to deal with than a small group of very different people.

Here's a hypothetical: You are an educator and trainer in the Information Technology (IT) industry and you are speaking to some prospects about teaching them how to run their lives and businesses from home. You want to persuade them that no matter how much they think they know, you could teach them stuff that will streamline their lives, give them more free time, and save them from wasting endless hours net-surfing inefficiently and not knowing how to deal with basic technical issues.

In the morning, you will go to the offices of a major corporation to speak to a group of new retirees who have taken lump sum payouts and are now dealing with the transition to a whole new phase of their lives. They are computer literate, but they only use the computer when they have to. Some of them may pay their bills online, but that's as sophisticated as they get. In the afternoon, you will go to a college campus speak to a group of snowboarding, goatee-sporting, baggy clothes-wearing, 22-year olds who are graduating from college. They each have created their own interactive website and they conduct much of their lives online.

Do you deliver the same presentation to both groups?

If you don't know a lot about your audience, large or small, let them lead the dance. Ask open-ended questions and encourage conversation. Then listen carefully, with all of your senses. If you listen long enough, people will let you know which issues are important to them, which issues to avoid, and what their favorite words and expressions are. You can also get an idea of the kinds of things they find humorous. Everything they do and say can help you. Listen to them. For instance:

- **Most people have a dominant, preferred sense**. Think of the last time you entered an unfamiliar house. What struck you first—the lighting, the size, the sounds, the smell? What did it feel like? The dominant sense is the one we will think about and do things with most often when given the choice. For example, recall the last new person you met. What comes to mind first, his/her name, face, or handshake?

  We each have a favorite sense with which we approach and process new information. Research in Neuro Linguistic Programming (NLP) has shown that most people are either visual, auditory, or kinesthetic (more on NLP in the next chapter). Here are some quick tips on how to determine who's who.

  Visual people (55 percent of population) tend to focus on pictures, colors, sizes, angles, contrasts of focus, and brightness. They tend to talk fast, think in pictures and charts, and prefer to be shown how to do new things. They often speak of how they "see" things ("looks good to me"). They pay careful attention to their appearance and the appearance of others. Their respiration is shallow and quick.

Auditory people (21 percent) focus on words, volume, cadence, inflection, pauses, pitch, and tempo. They are good at handling people, are open to both sides of an argument, and like good questions. They think in language, talk about how things sound ("sounds good to me") and are dominators of conversations. Background noises can either bug or help them. If you want them to do something, you should explain it to them (not show them or give them written instructions). They breathe deeply and speak rhythmically.

Kinesthetic people (24 percent) focus on feelings, texture, vibration, intensity, pressure, tension, and movement. What they perceive is often a reflection of their feelings. They are touchers and they judge situations and people by how they make them feel inside ("that doesn't feel right to me"). They breathe deeply and slowly, are more patient than the other types, and they speak slower and lower. Because they take most of their cues from their feelings, they are more prone to moodiness.

• **Predictability**

Once you know, from observation, how a person looks at the world, you are in a better position to effectively and efficiently communicate with them. You are also in a better position to predict their behavior. Think about it: You have two friends who are similar in a lot of ways and share many of the same interests. For instance, they both like to fish. However one prefers fly-fishing while the other prefers spear fishing. Who do you think has more patience?

There are other useful ways to look at the way we represent and process what is around us. For instance, are you someone who looks for the similarities between things or focuses on the differences? Think of the last two dates you were on or the last two cars you had (and please infer nothing from my choice of those examples). Take a moment to jot a few descriptive phrases about them in relation to each other. Look at the language you used. If you want to get an idea of whether someone looks for similarities or differences, pay attention to their language of comparison. If that opportunity doesn't arise, ask them to compare their last two cars.

My only caveat when noting that someone seems to be visual and then tailoring all of your verbiage to include phrases such as: "How do you see it?" is to be careful. Humans don't like when things aren't predictable. We have a strong urge to try to reduce uncertainty. These categories are not absolutes and should not be used to judge anyone or put them in a mental box, along with others whom you have deemed to belong there. Prediction, explanation, and understanding can help us reduce uncertainty, but they can also *give the illusion* of reducing uncertainty. You might want to *begin* by using a category, but don't use it as an excuse to stop looking for clues.

Determining how someone looks at the world or processes information helps you to understand them and it gives you a clue about how they like to hear new information. For people in sales (read: anyone trying to convince anyone else of anything), this is very important because people tend to like, and buy from, people who are like them.

- Actionable

Actionable is a term used often in motivational circles. You have probably heard that you should aim to empower your audience: to make them feel able to do whatever it is they need or want to do. Actionable is the logical next step, you empower them toward specific action. Don't just motivate them to get up and go, motivate them to get up and do. The Self-Discovery Exercises in this book make it actionable. The essence of The *Communication Essentials* is not mere explanation, but explanation intended—*and designed*—to get you to try to improve the way you communicate.

Working at Becoming a Better Listener

Listening is the delicate balance of silence and response. The response should be both verbal and nonverbal, and should indicate acknowledgment, understanding, and compassion. Acknowledgment can be in the form of an "uh-huh," an "I see," or just leaning forward, nodding your head, and looking into the speaker's eye with a silence that says, "You have my complete attention."

Most people manage to quickly demonstrate that they are listening. However, many feel the compulsion to verbally respond in some way as soon as the speaker takes a breath. This response comes in the form of either unwanted advice or an immediate agreement, disagreement, or judgment, when all the speaker wanted was to be heard.

When it is done properly, listening builds the self-esteem of the speaker, who feels validated as a result. In *Orbiting the Giant Hairball: A Corporate Fool's Guide to Surviving With Grace*, author Gordon MacKenzie refers to the state of "compassionate emptiness" he assumes when listening. He says, "I ...imagine myself to be an empty vessel existing only to receive. As fully as possible. Without judgment (210)."

If you want to observe a topnotch example of listening, watch Oprah Winfrey. When Oprah is listening to her guests, they know it—they *feel* it. I know this because *I can actually feel her listening to someone else, through my television!* The next time Oprah is on, look at her face, particularly her eyes. Notice her body language. Listen to her words and see what they elicit in whomever she is speaking to. Watch how the guest actually becomes involved in the way Oprah listens, even when she doesn't say anything. They feel her compassion and they appreciate it.

Self-Discovery Exercise #3: Listening

If you would like to improve your listening, I suggest you begin by *listening to yourself.* The best way to do this is not to focus on what you (think you) said and how (you think) it sounded, but to listen, with all of your senses. Your intention should be to attend to *how others respond and react to you.* They will tell you how you really came across.

The microcassette recorder will once again be useful. If you are thinking "Why? It's not as if I can hear myself listening!" that's not really true. Listen for your pauses: where do they occur and what happens immediately before and after them? And most important, listen to *your listeners.* Do your listeners have to constantly repeat or paraphrase themselves? Do your responses to their words correspond to what they have just said, or do they sound more like brilliant statements you were developing while they were speaking, and you were just waiting for the moment you could debut them?

You can also ask your buddy about your ability to listen. Your listening capacity (as well as your desire to listen) usually varies depending on your audience and the situation, so keep in mind that your buddy's assessment could very well be unique to that relationship. Write all of your responses and reactions in section three of your five-subject notebook. Your comments will tell you what you need to improve.

A sure way to improve your listening is to practice. Go to a lecture on something you don't know anything about, or go to a lecture about something *you think you don't like* or want to hear about. Think about listening. And live by The Golden Rule of Listening: Listen the way you would want someone to listen to you.

Troubleshooting

- If you feel like you are doing everything you can do, yet your message still isn't being heard, be mindful of how *you* are contributing to that frustrating situation. Begin by simply asking your audience to paraphrase what you have said. Paraphrasing, by definition, will involve the use of words that are different from the words originally used. That alone tells you something about the listener and where they're coming from. The more they talk, the more clues they are giving you, and the better you will be able to tailor your message thereafter.

There are at least two people involved in a communication: the speaker and the listener (sender and receiver, if you prefer). Both have emotional sensitivities that originated in childhood and that color the way they look at the world and phrase their thoughts. If you are paying attention, you will find that most people are continuously giving you information about how they want to be spoken to and dealt with. The next chapter will detail how to decode some of the nonverbal clues and signals others are emitting, and how to achieve a heightened sense of awareness about the messages you are sending, consciously and otherwise.

- Remember that what immediately irks us about others is likely to be what we find most unsavory about ourselves. Therefore, if you have an immediate, visceral reaction to either something someone has said or to the actual person doing the talking (and that is an important distinction), before you react, consider whether the origin of your feeling is really within you.

A Note on What You See

Have you noticed that whenever the neighbors of a serial killer or mass murderer are interviewed, they all say the same thing: "He seemed like such a nice, normal guy." Do you ask yourself, "What is wrong with those people? How could they overlook all of the oddities in his behavior?" I used to quietly ridicule the parents, neighbors, and friends of those people and wonder how they only saw the goodness. Then I realized they were seeing things that really were there, and simply (and unconsciously) choosing not to see anything that didn't fit in the paradigm of kindness and goodness. After all, what parent would want to look for signs that their child was a serial killer? Would you?

Seeing is very much like listening; we see what we expect to see. It's called The Law of the Lens. In order to see what is really around us and not just what we want to see, we have to re-learn what it means to look. We have to attempt to be conscious of things around us that we haven't noticed before. We cannot possibly process all of the stimuli around us all of the time, so we selectively attend to things. Just as with listening, we will alter reality and see it in a way that is more in line with our expectations and past experiences. The best strategy to prevent this from happening is to be as mindful as you can, and check your observations with others.

Summary
- The purpose of listening is to understand in an empathic way. Listening is not about judging or mocking.
- Listening in silence is rarely a bad idea.
- Reflect on the words, tones, and situations that trigger your emotions. Remember that if you allow your emotions to be triggered, you are likely to miss (or worse, mishear) what a speaker is saying to you.
- General guidelines to follow:
- The more appealing you are to your listeners, the more they like you and the more they listen to you.
  - The more memorable you are as a speaker, the more people will listen. Being memorable includes being funny and creative.
  - The more meaningful your material is to your audience, the better the chance that they will listen carefully to you.
  - Most people have a preferred sense. Determine what that sense is and present yourself and your material in a way that caters to that sense.
  - Be actionable. Give your audience something specific they can do to make your material sink in.
  - If there appears to be a problem, reflect on how you could be contributing to that situation. If it is not clear to you, ask someone in your audience what you can do to help them understand you better.

CHAPTER FIVE

What You Look Like

The most effective way to persuade someone is to use the same "programming" that he processes information with. When one computer communicates with another via a communications device, it is difficult for them to transmit and receive messages if they don't run on the same system (software). Similarly, we will need to match our counterparts' values, beliefs, attitudes, and especially their meta-programs if we are to be completely effective in the persuasion process (Hogan, 245).

No one cannot not communicate (read it again; I promise it makes sense). Everyone is giving off a constant, uninterrupted stream of non-verbal signals that tells you about what they are thinking and feeling. The same is true for you. Therefore, it behooves you to evaluate whether your nonverbal communication is consistent with what you want people to see.

This is not going to be a crash course in eye movement and body language in an attempt to program you to perfect certain gestures and eliminate others. In fact, there is a popular movement called Neuro Linguistic Programming, which was introduced in the United States in the 1970s and focuses on teaching its students how to improve their relationships by understanding how people transmit and receive information through their senses. The techniques largely involve the study and interpretation of gestures. NLP provides labels for what we do when we are relating to others and teaches us how we can optimize our effectiveness. There are plenty of books on NLP in your local library and your local bookstore. There are also several websites dedicated to it.

This book, however, is a review of the conventional wisdom about nonverbal communication, including some principles discussed in NLP, with the ever-present caveat that *there are plenty of exceptions.* And rather than teaching you what to do and what not to do in order to manipulate others, I'd like to use this chapter to address

Impression Management. I'm assuming that your motives are positive and productive; I want to make sure that is the message you are sending. Again, this isn't about learning how to fake the mannerisms for optimal probability of persuasion, or judging others according to their body language. Impression management involves all of your senses, and focuses on how to send the message you intend to send and make certain it is heard. It involves *everything* you are doing when you are speaking to an audience of one or one hundred.

Everything?

Yes, everything someone else can see, hear, or feel, that is coming from you, *and even some things that are coming from them that you have triggered.* I include the latter because, if you know enough about your audience you can predict their behavior and the things that are likely to trigger them. This includes the obvious and the not-so-obvious. For instance, did you know that of our senses, the one that triggers feelings and memories the fastest, is the sense of smell? Scents are so powerful that they can actually affect our mood (pass by the bakery where your favorite smell from childhood is wafting out of the door and try not to be in a good mood), our ability to concentrate (peppermint helps), and our ability to feel aroused. The current research on aromatherapy shows, believe it or not, that men respond (read: become aroused) in the presence of the scents of cinnamon and pumpkin pie, whereas women prefer licorice. The last time I said this to a large group of people, the local candy store had a run on Good and Plenty.

Some of the things that come from you that affect others are in your control, and others don't appear to be. Emotions, for instance, begin internally. Then they produce physiological changes that occur in the human body that tend to produce predictable outer manifestations of those emotions. Here are a few examples of this phenomenon.

• Anger

When you are angry your heart and breathing rates jump, your blood flows to your hands in preparation to hit something, and your overall energy increases. The volume and projection of your voice also increase in order to attempt to instill fear in your listeners.

• Fear

When you are in fear, your heart and breathing speed up as well, but your blood takes a different direction; it leaves your face and surges to your legs for a quick escape (the flight portion of Fight or Flight—see above for the fight part). Momentarily, your body freezes, making it possible to determine if hiding would be better than running. The volume and projection of your voice lessen to minimize the potential of drawing attention.

- **Disgust**

Disgust is usually indicated by the shunning of your senses. For instance, your eyes squint, your face turns away, your lips curl, and your nose wrinkles. Your vocalization becomes staccato and is marked by quick, short outbursts of breath, similar to what you do when you spit out unwanted food.

- **Love**

Love is a relaxed state marked by increasing blood flow to the lips and hands accompanied by an open physical bearing and deep breathing, which facilitate arousal, contentment, and cooperation. Vocalization becomes more resonant, perhaps to soothe and charm.

What You Can Control

With some education and training you can control your emotions and their corresponding physical manifestations. That will take some time. However, there are other gestures and reactions that you can control *starting now*. Remember the earlier discussion about your message being "actionable?" I have gathered the following tips from observing and studying the interpersonal human experience, inside the boardroom, inside the classroom, and even on the subway. Whether you are dealing with a large or small audience, all of these tips will apply. Controlling these behaviors takes practice, but you will begin to improve as soon as you put your attention on them.

Each person has certain physical movements that often can translate into attitudes and, occasionally, words. However, body movements of one person can, and often do, mean totally different things when compared to the same movement of another person. Unless you know the person very well you cannot put a label on his behavior.

Nodding

I begin with nodding so that you'll remember it (we tend to recall the first and last items in a list faster than the others). Many people don't even address nodding when talking about gestures and what they mean. Instead, they concentrate on your eyes and your hands. But the nod is a powerful sign and a powerful tool, and because you probably nod more than you know, it's a good idea to examine how that is making other people feel. Here are some tips about nodding:

- There are three types of nods: the single, the double, and the triple.
  1. The Single: When you are listening and you nod once, the speaker's behavior will probably not be altered. The Single acts to sustain the interaction without interrupting it. (Exception: The understanding nod is treated as

58

encouraging when it happens simultaneous with speaker's message, words, and content. When it is out of sync, it expresses a lack of attention and involvement where one is beating time to the pulse of their own anxiety rather than the rhythm of the speaker.)

2. The Double: The Double is like a single at times, but at others it will cause the speaker to change their tone or elaborate a point.

3. The Triple: The Triple is associated with a dramatic change in the other person's behavior and usually causes a vocal hesitation, a change in subject, or a fading away of tone of the speaker. The Triple seems to produce a mild level of anxiety in the speaker, either about the content or the presentation of their message. Because The Triple is all that the speaker has to go on, he usually finds a way to check out of the conversation. If that is not the effect you desire, be careful when you nod.

4. The speed of all of the nods is also important. Quick nods act as a strong affirmation, while slow ones are likely to interrupt the flow of speech.

5. Nodding combinations:

    •   Nodding and smiling. When you ask a question, if your listener is nodding and smiling, they can't wait to answer your question. You've hit gold for them.

    •   Nodding and pausing. When you ask a question and your listener nods and pauses (particularly if pausing is not ordinarily in their pattern), and if their voice gets lower as well, you can probably predict that the question is better than the answer. (You can also predict that when someone says, "That's a good question," the question is sure to be better than the answer you're about to get.)

    •   The next time you want someone to agree with you, as you ask them a question nod your head. Observe as it becomes difficult for them to say no.

Hand Gestures

1. Do not point your finger at someone when you are speaking. It is perceived as a rude and hostile gesture. You probably want to eliminate any gestures that look like you learned them in a karate, boxing, or judo class, as well.

    Bill Clinton was a thruster (no pun intended). He was incapable of saying the name Ken Starr without pointing and thrusting his finger. His famous *mea culpa* speech was so carefully staged and filmed (with a tight camera angle), that you couldn't even see his hands, except when they went to his face to wipe his tears. How's that for manipulation!

2. Do not rub your hands when talking about money. Why not? Go to a mirror right now and look at yourself while you rub your hands together. Don't you look greedy? Is that what you want people to think?

3. Desmond Morris, author of *The Naked Ape: A Zoologist's Study of the Human Animal*, talks about our primitive and instinctive movements of our hands toward our faces. He says they transmit signals to others that we are having difficulty processing what they are saying.

   Remember the three monkeys: see no evil, hear no evil, and speak no evil? As a child, when you didn't want to face/see something, what did you do? I bet you covered your eyes. And if you didn't want to hear something, did you cover your ears? And if you were afraid of saying something due to the probable consequences, did you cover your mouth?

   As adults, we use the same three gestures, only much more subtly and unconsciously. For instance, when most people have just heard something they do not believe they tend to move their hands toward their face, perhaps rubbing their eye or under it, or scratching their nose or lip area.

   So if you see someone moving their hands toward their face in any of these ways they might not understand or believe what you have said. To confirm you are being understood, all you have to do is ask if they have any questions. You can also ask them to explain what they believe you said.

4. When your hands are moving they should not just be flailing around randomly. If you are going to talk with your hands, your hands should be saying something that could be understood even if you weren't speaking. Refraining from unnecessary hand movements is difficult for most people but worth practicing. Hand movements that don't match what you are saying are not only distracting, but they are misleading.

   Here's an exercise: Say the following sentence and use what you think are appropriate gestures.

   The little boy is about this tall; he comes up to my waist.

   The only necessary, descriptive gesture would be to put your hand or hands by your waist to indicate the height of the boy. Anything else is extraneous and distracting.

   Richard Nixon was an example of a person whose gesturing got him into trouble. Many people did not trust him when he spoke but they couldn't quite articulate their reasons. Nixon's problem was that he would say something like, "We will take care of..." and *after* he said it he would pound his fist on the table. *Hand gestures should occur simultaneously with the spoken words.* When they occur after the words, they give the impression of insincerity.

If you want to find out if your gestures are ineffective or you talk with our hands a lot yet they aren't saying much, ask your trusted friend to pay attention to you for a week or so. In addition, if presentations to any size audience are a part of your life, videotaping yourself is worth the expense. Most people do not realize how and how much they use their hands. And because most people have developed their hand-gesture habits over the course of their lifetime, those habits tend to be difficult to break. A way to make it easier is to ask someone who is with you often (a co-worker, your spouse) to remind you to use your hands only for emphasis or description.

5. People who want to dominate use larger gestures and direct those gestures away from their body. The dominant person speaks more overall, and looks at you more when they are speaking and less when you are speaking. The percentage of time spent looking at someone who is talking is a nonverbal, subconscious way of establishing control.

Eyes

We call the eyes the windows to the soul for a good reason; they speak very clearly about our degree of interest, disbelief, and trust. They let us know if we are building rapport or if we need to alter what we are saying or how we are saying it. It has been said that Aristotle Onassis always wore sunglasses during negotiations so that his eyes could not be caught leaking information. The reason was probably that he knew that our pupils automatically dilate when we are excited. Here are some other tips to watch out for...

- Blinking—When someone is very interested in what you are saying they blink very few times. They will give you a big blink at the end of what you have said as if to underscore the period of the sentence. When someone does not believe what you are saying or has no interest, they will indicate this with a series of rapid blinks.
- Pupils—When someone is interested in you their pupils will dilate. It is subtle but very telling because it cannot be faked. Professional card players often wear tinted glasses so that other players cannot read the excitement in their eyes. Babies have large dilated pupils. It is nature's way of saying "Hold me," "Pick me up," "I love you."

Of course, when you go to a restaurant for a romantic candlelit dinner, don't confuse your date's dilated pupils with how they feel about you; they just can't see the menu. Also remember that pupils have a function other than to demonstrate interest. For example, when you are under stress your pupils will get smaller. This is a primitive reaction that allows for more acute vision, presumably to better see the saber-toothed tiger/sport utility vehicle coming directly at you.

- Eye Contact—How do you feel when you are talking to someone and their eyes are darting all over, as if they're looking for something better to attend to? In our culture we have words for people who don't look you in the eye (e.g., shifty). If you don't want to say hello to someone you know or you don't want to pick up a hitchhiker, what do you do? Look the other way.

  Looking into the eyes of the person to whom you are speaking is an important way of letting them know that you are indeed paying attention to what they are saying. When I say looking, I don't mean staring without a break; such eye contact is rude and tells the speaker that you are probably zoning out and bored with what they are saying.

  When you do break eye contact, when you are approaching that moment where there is too much contact, it is important to break it downwards rather than sideways. Sideways indicates extreme disinterest. Think about this: When someone breaks eye contact and looks to the side, and then you immediately look to the side as well to see what they are looking at (read: who just walked into the bar), how does that make you feel?

  If you are giving a presentation to a group you should look in all directions throughout the presentation. Face one person at a time and complete a thought while looking at that person. Then, face another and make another point. And when you are asked a question, look directly at the person who asked the question and move toward them. The toward movement indicates interest.

Incongruence

Signs of incongruence are usually indications of insincerity or lying. If you are saying something and your face or your body is sending a message that is not consistent with your words, your listener will not necessarily accuse you of lying, but they are probably uneasy about you and/or what you have said. If people flat out said "I don't believe you," we'd all be better off. But that doesn't ordinarily happen. The more typical chain of events is: You say "You can trust me" and then immediately smile and lift your brow. Your listener, who should be running by now, remains and says nothing, yet feels like there was something off about your message. Regardless of how sincere you may have been, your message was that you cannot be trusted. There are usually several signs that tell others we are not being sincere.

As a rule (to which there are exceptions), strong emotions usually appear on the face *before* vocalization. Further, sincere displays of emotion are usually symmetrical; both sides of the face smile, both eyebrows go up, etc. The mismatch of words and body language or facial expression speaks volumes to those who are paying attention, and it also speaks, albeit more vaguely, to those who are not looking for it. For example, if someone says "yes" or "okay" with a softer voice than the rest of their conversation, or if their "yes" is accompanied by a suddenly tense forehead, or a break in eye contact, you will probably wonder about the sincerity of the "yes," although you might not know why.

Dr. Paul Ekman has trained customs officials and police in how to tell if someone is lying. He observed videos and isolated a group of gestures and movements that accurately (more than 90 percent) informed him that the subject was lying. Again, incongruity is the key. It can reveal itself in the voice, the face, and/or the emotions. For instance, when a person's eyes close for an extra long time, that tells us that they need extra time to figure something out. In addition, microfacial expressions (quick expressions of a person's true emotions that they display without being aware), such as a mini shrug, particularly in conjunction with a tense forehead, could indicate lying. A fleeting grimace or a sudden drop in voice could indicate lying as well. And the carotid artery often pulses and the eyes wander and blink rapidly when a person is not telling the truth.

Experts call the signal that the subject is lying, "The Tell." For example, two cops are trying to determine if a subject is lying. Cop A tells the subject that when Cop B comes into the room to tell Cop B that he (Cop A) is moving his car. Cop A tells the subject that he is actually going for donuts; what the subject is instructed to tell Cop B is a lie. Cop B comes in and says where's Cop A. Just before the subject lies, he clears his throat—that is The Tell.

Self-Discovery #4: Nonverbal Language

You might think that your trusty microcassette recorder will be of no use for this section. However, if you tape your conversations and presentations, and listen carefully to the responses to what you say, remember that 55 percent of those responses are to your nonverbal behavior. Unless you also videotape yourself, though, you may not recall exactly what you did to get the responses you got. This is why I suggest that, for a week, you rehearse your important conversations and your presentations in front of a mirror. Look at your natural body language first and then alter it so it is meaningful rather than random.

Make your gestures speak. If you rehearse and are mindful of your gestures, when you listen to your recordings you will have an idea of what it is you did to get the responses you got.

In addition, ask your buddy for feedback on your body language. I recommend doing this *before* they see this chapter (the power of suggestion can produce some interesting results), at least once, and then after reading this chapter. Write your comments and reactions in the fourth section of your five-subject notebook.

Your entries in this section will tell you about the congruence between the messages received and your original intentions. If there is a lack of congruence, you probably need to attend to and alter your body language. This is more difficult than the other areas of communication because so much of it is unconscious. After some practice you might be able to get your eye contact and nodding under control. Meanwhile, your hands and your feet, which are the vehicles for much of the leakage of your real feelings, could be creating incongruence. To your audience incongruence is tantamount to insincerity.

What You Can Do

As I have discussed previously, the first thing to do in any communication situation is decide what it is you want your message to be. This is known as your intention. Next, you need to consider your audience. Virtually everything you know about your audience can help you to formulate your message in the way that is most likely to be grasped by them.

Your objective is to be as likeable as possible to your audience because people tend to trust those they like. The foundation of trust enables people to open up, share information, support each other, and speak honestly. Trust is like readiness for unguarded interaction. Imagine running into a large, growling dog. That's a guarded interaction. Unguarded is the opposite.

If people tend to like people who are like them, the way to achieve your objective of likeability is to observe your audience and mirror their behavior and language. The more you know about your audience, the better position you are in to make them feel comfortable by speaking, acting, and looking in a way that is similar to the way they speak, act, and look. You will also find that you will begin to actually feel in a way that is similar to them by assuming their physiology. This is what empathy is all about.

Knowing your audience

In order to most effectively communicate with someone, it helps if you know what they are motivated by. Every major bookstore has shelves of books that propose systems for personality analysis and categorization. Each school of therapy has a different perspective on what is important and how to achieve clarity and resolution in relationships. And popular magazines regularly publish quizzes by the personality-guru-of-the-moment, whose system will help improve your business and personal relationships.

I studied many of the old standards, such as the Myers Briggs personality type indicator, which, incidentally, informs me that I am an ENFP (Extroverted, Intuiting, Feeling, Perceiving). And I am up-to-speed on color theories (I am Red, according to Taylor Hartman, Ph.D's, *The Color Code* and Green according to Carol Ritberger, Ph.D.'s *What Color is Your Personality?*). My primary mode of processing information is Visual (as opposed to Auditory or Kinesthetic: see any NLP text for an exercise that will help you determine what your preferred mode is; you might be surprised). According to Virginia Satir's system of common verbal behavioral patterns (The Placater, The Blamer, The Computer, The Distracter, and The Leveler) I am a Distracter.

Personally, I can't seem to bypass an opportunity to discover a new way to categorize myself and those around me. I find such things entertaining and enlightening. Each of the above labels tells you something about me, and all of them together actually give you a pretty good idea of how I deal with things and what is most important to me. They each approach who I am from a different angle, yet they also overlap somewhat. You now have more information about me than you do about many people you see every day. However, getting to know *myself* is one thing—but categorizing *others* and playing amateur psychologist with them, particularly without a lot evidence, is another story altogether.

Unless you administer the necessary testing instruments, it is difficult to determine, with certainty, what someone you do not know very well is about. Knowledge of the various theories cannot hurt, but it is not a substitute for paying attention, asking questions, listening to the other person, and listening to your intuition. If you hone all of these skills you will probably find less of a need to look for ways to categorize. Instead, you will be able to develop a customized way to deal with each person, respecting their individuality.

Summary

- Everyone is giving off a constant, uninterrupted stream of nonverbal signals that tells you about what they are thinking and feeling.
- Impression management involves making certain the message you intend to send is the one you do send, and that it is heard by your audience.
- Emotions produce physiological changes in the human body that are predictable. With education and training, you can

control your emotions and their corresponding physical manifestations.

- The way you nod and use your hands speak quietly but strongly about what you are really thinking and feeling.
- Your eye movements and eye contact communicate strongly, as well. They are more difficult, and in some cases, impossible to control.
- When your eyes or hands send a message that is different from your verbal message, your listener might not know that for certain or have any evidence that you are not being sincere, but they will feel the incongruity.
- As a speaker, you can help improve the listening of your audience by presenting yourself and your material in a way that caters to their likes. Essentially, the more you are like them, the more they will listen to you (and like you).

CHAPTER SIX

The Invisibles
Humor, Intuition, and Creative Thinking

The most successful communicators I know are also the most creative people I know. Though some of them are also talented at expressing themselves artistically, that's not the creativity I am referring to. In this instance, when I use the word "creative," I mean the ability to solve problems, resolve conflict, and generally deal with adversity, all in a unique and outside-the-box kind of way. These creative people have what I like to call a healthy disrespect for conventional wisdom. They listen to their intuition, they don't follow the pack, they have their own, well-thought out reasons for doing what they do (although this often does not appear to be the case to the untrained eye), and they share an offbeat, slightly twisted sense of humor.

When faced with a moment of adversity, these people see anything but. They view every situation as a learning opportunity, with adverse conditions being responsible for more learning than any situation that goes swimmingly. After all, if nothing is going awry, there is no reason to try to come up with a creative solution. However, and this is what is most extraordinary about them, they thrive on the excitement and fun of finding alternatives *even when they don't have to—even when there is no problem.*

We can all hope to become more successful, but without a plan, we are left with only that hope. You should be at the final section of your five-subject notebook now, and as usual, you should take stock of where you are. The three main topics of this chapter are humor, intuition, and creative thinking. They are difficult to evaluate, which is part of the reason why I call them the invisibles.

Humor

Self-Discovery #5a

Your sense of humor is probably the easiest invisible to describe—paying attention is all it takes. Over the next week or so, reflect on:

- What you think is funny and why.
- How your sense of humor manifests itself (e.g., Are you witty or do you prefer slapstick? Are you the subject of your humor, or are others?)
- In what situations do you use humor the most?
- The reactions of others. Do other people seem to appreciate your sense of humor?

Once again, if you cannot figure out the answer to any of these questions, ask your buddy. This area may be a bit more sensitive than others, because we all like to think that we are funny in our own way, and asking someone their opinion of our sense of humor creates a vulnerability most of us would rather avoid. This is why I recommend that if you want feedback from anyone, ask them to *describe* your sense of humor, *not to judge it.* Judgment is where problems begin and emotions flare up.

A helpful technique for describing your sense of humor is to ask someone to compare it to a sitcom or a comedian *that you are fond of.* This allows them to let you know how you come across while buffering any blows because you are no longer the subject. For instance, I did this exercise with my friend Stacy, who is a well-educated professional, but a bit on the uppity side. I compared her sense of humor to that of Dennis Miller. She likes Dennis Miller, I like Dennis Miller, so she knows she isn't on the defensive. Therefore, when I describe Dennis Miller as a comedian who often doesn't have mass appeal because many of his references are so esoteric that only *he* sees the humor in them, Stacy is not upset. In fact, she is perversely complimented, and she gets the point that she should be more attentive to the experiences and educations of her listeners.

Something a bit more ambiguous happened to me many years ago, around the time the movie "10" was popular and I was a brazen youth. A gentleman I had recently met told me I looked like the woman from "10." "Bo Derek?" I responded, flattered and pleased. "No, the other one." "Oh, Julie Andrews." Okay, so I figured I had a bit of work to do on my image, but things could be worse. I mean, I do kind of look like her.

Then he says, "but you remind me of someone else ..." I, naturally, am thinking along the lines of Audrey Hepburn or Ingrid Bergman. In their thirties, of course. But then the name that had previously escaped him suddenly surfaces and, excited and astounded by the similarities, he says, "That's it—I figured it out! You remind me of Rodney Dangerfield! It's like, you're *Ronni* Dangerfield!" Now, call me crazy, but I'm not so sure if that was a compliment, and I would have preferred if he had stopped at the comparison to Julie Andrews. Our subsequent conversation was a bit strained.

The reason for using only positive comparisons is that if someone senses they are being insulted they will then look to be insulted, and anything you say will either be distorted or fall on deaf ears. I've heard stories of fights that started between friends because they misunderstood this exercise. A popular scenario makes this point: A young, male stockbroker asks his girlfriend, whom he trusts implicitly, to assist him with putting some kind name to his sense of humor so he can get a handle on how the world sees him. Naturally, he thinks he's quite funny. *Most people think they are quite funny.* So he asks his girlfriend, and she comes up with—"You know that Andrew Dice Clay guy?" Whether or not he thinks Andrew Dice Clay is funny is immaterial, because he knows that she can't stand him. Therefore, anything she says thereafter is useless, because in his mind, she thinks he's a buffoon.

Developing Your Funny Bone

By choosing to develop our capacity for humor, fun, and laughter, we exert a direct, biochemical effect on our overall wellness by making our fears manageable and sustaining our hopes" (Metcalf 13).

Remember the movie *Arthur*, with Dudley Moore and Liza Minelli (and if you don't, rent it this weekend)? One of my many favorite scenes was when Dudley Moore started laughing for no apparent reason. People looked at him like he was nuts, which he was, but that's not the point. His explanation was simply, "Sometimes I just think funny thoughts." There's a guy who knows how to live.

If you don't think that humor is appropriate or necessary in your professional life, try this statistic on for size: People remember less than 10 percent of what you say, but almost all of the jokes. Maybe they can't go on to tell them with the same flare or impeccable timing, but they certainly remember that someone made them laugh.

Humor is a powerful tool for keeping people's attention and helping them with their *retention* of what you have said. My recommendation is to incorporate humor whenever you can—even at work. Whatever your career involves, you should take it seriously, but whatever you do, don't take yourself too seriously!

Humor is a cherished part of my everyday life and I believe it is necessary for my survival and continued (alleged) sanity. Much to my surprise, however, this was the most arduous part of this book to compose, because I had a difficult time describing what I think humor is, how I think it works, and how it can be developed. Fortunately, I was able to garner a lot of help from various experts on the subject.

Ironically (or not, if you really think about it), research on humor is not funny business. Although there are far more books on nonverbal communication and verbal communication than on humor, there are several real gems that I recommend. Sam Horn's *Tongue Fu! How to Deflect, Disarm, and Defuse Any Verbal Conflict,* Allen Klein's *The Healing Power of Humor: Techniques for Getting Through Loss, Setbacks, Upsets, Disappointments, Difficulties, Trials, Tribulations, and All That Not-So-Funny Stuff,* and the often ridiculous C.W. Metcalf and Roma Felible's *Lighten Up.* Klein talks about joke-jitsu (which, when correctly employed, can turn any disadvantage into an advantage), Horn talks about Fun Fu! Tongue Glue (use your imagination), and lists of Words to Use and Words to Lose, and Metcalf's humaerobics are some of the silliest, yet effective exercises I've ever used. Jordan Ayan's *Aha! 10 Ways to Free Your Creative Spirit and Find Your Great Ideas* will help you assess your "humor quotient," among other things, and is a great resource for anyone wanting to explore ways to increase their creative flow.

Metcalf calls humor, "a set of survival skills that relieve tension, keeping us fluid and flexible instead of allowing us to become rigid and breakable in the face of relentless change" (9). He frequently discusses his discontent with our culture, which "believes our problems can be beaten only if we just get tough enough, work a little harder, and get really serious!" (7).

Metcalf's mission is to combat what he calls Terminal Professionalism. Terminal Professionalism is "an odd disease...that some people actually seem proud of having. These are people who will say, 'Now pay attention; I'm dead serious!' After a decade studying and consulting with companies throughout the world, I've become convinced that in a global economy characterized by ever-accelerating change, the failure to nourish and encourage lightness in the workplace not only undermines productivity, creativity, adaptability, and morale—it literally *drives people crazy!*" (148).

Metcalf's plan to eradicate Terminal Professionalism includes the regular practice of "humaerobics," a set of physical and mental exercises designed to enhance humor skills and help you take yourself lightly. They include developing a humor library, laughing at your naked self in a full-length mirror, and making a face that is so silly that it gets an enormous belly laugh, without fail, from all of my friends.

The Healing Power of Humor
"Here, as in Japan, stress has become the new red badge of courage among many hardworking, ambitious Americans—or, at least, management tends to reward those who see it that way. How sick can you get, and keep coming to work—now that's professional! How 'bout that Henderson guy, eh? Massive heart attack and triple bypass surgery last night, but, he's hooked up to his IV at his desk and is dictating letters. What a pro" (Metcalf, 158-9).

The only undeniable truth about humor, and particularly about laughter, is that it is good for you. And I don't mean that in some kind

70

of New Agey good-for-the-soul way; I mean it actually improves your health and longevity.

Norman Cousins, pioneer of the research on humor, discovered that laughter actually stimulates the release of endorphins, which, among other things, makes you sharper and better able to retain information. It also relaxes muscles, lowers blood pressure, suppresses stress-related hormones, and enhances the functioning of the immune system. And laughter helps open up other options so you can see more alternatives.

What are You Laughing At?

Humor is subjective. Any attempt at qualifying and quantifying what is funny is futile. Fortunately, though, humor is not necessarily an innate quality. Sure, some people are just plain funnier than the rest of us. No matter how much coaching I get and how much I practice, I realize that I will never be as funny as Robin Williams. But that doesn't mean I shouldn't try to be the funniest Ronni Burns I can be.

So what do I think is funny? *Where do I find humor?* Where should you look to find humor? Everywhere. Just look around you; so much of our lives is ironic and even absurd. While I think some jokes are funny, jokes are such a small part of humor. And the ones that you will find the funniest are probably the ones that are closest to you. For instance, three of my personal favorite one-liners are:

> If all economists were layered end to end, they wouldn't reach a conclusion.

> Why did god create economists? To make weather forecasters look good.

> What's the significance of April 15th? It's the day most people find out their mutual funds are taxable.

Now that's funny stuff. To me. And it's such a hoot because of the irony. There is a great definition of irony in Allen Klein's *The Healing Power of Humor:* "to find irony, you need to look at the relationship of how something started out and how it wound up" (71). My friend Mikki sent flowers to the grand opening of a store of one of her largest customers. The florist sent a card that said "Rest In Peace." Meanwhile, someone in a funeral home somewhere received an arrangement that said "Good Luck in Your New Location."

Some great examples of irony are newspaper headlines. Don Connelly of Putnum Funds found the following within a month of each other.

IBM Continues Comeback ...IBM in The Tank

Used Car Market Hits Pothole...Used Car Market Leads Industry in Sales

Oil Stocks Grease Gains ...Oil Stocks Tank

Dow Sinks 94-Renewed Inflation Fears ...Dow Soars-Low Inflation Confirmed

And how about bumper stickers ....

Wisdom is learning what to ignore

Potential has a shelf life

If less is more, there is no end to you

Keep an open mind, but not so open that your brains fall out

Experience is what you get when you don't get what you want

Take the high road, there's a lot less traffic

My other favorite source of one-liners is the great Yogi Berra. The following still make me chuckle every time I hear/read them.

A nickel ain't worth a dime anymore.

Why buy good luggage when you only use it when you travel?

When you get to a fork in the road, take it.

Ninety percent of the game is half mental.

That restaurant has gotten so popular no one goes there anymore.

If you don't go to other people's funerals they won't go to yours.

Looking at adversity from a different angle can also produce some pretty funny stuff. How about this: As popular motivational speaker

Joel Weldon says, "When competition undercuts you with price and says 'We Have $5 Haircuts,' how about using 'We Fix $5 Haircuts' as your slogan."

Humor lets you take a situation and reframe it to give you more options. For example, every now and then when I am stuck in traffic, late for an appointment and starting to feel very stressed, I reframe my situation. I decide that I am a very famous person in a motorcade. I open my sunroof and sit very tall and wave that artificial wave that politicians use. You know, the one that looks more like they are screwing in a light bulb than saying a sincere "hi." It works remarkably well and gives me a chuckle every time. In *Making Things Better by Making Them Worse*, author Alan Fay notes that when you exaggerate a stressful situation to the point of ridiculousness, it is a lot easier to put it into perspective and to find other ways of coping.

Bad Humor, Good Humor

"Safe humor (like safe sex) is 100 percent safe only when you abstain or stick to yourself as the subject" (Metcalf, 174).

Humor can build or destroy trust. There are some jokes that are probably safe any time in any company (e.g., I can probably go into a room of men and women and say, "When a man says there are only two minutes left in a football game, it's the same amount of time as when a woman says I'll be ready in two minutes." It's a safe joke because everyone gets mocked and everyone sees the truth of it). However, most humor and jocularity should be delivered with sensitivity to the audience and sensitivity to time.

Sensitivity to audience simply means that there are just some things that you don't want to say to certain people. Usually, you know what those things are/might be and you steer clear of them. But when you don't know what irks your audience, always err on the side of caution. Your hilariously funny joke may become your biggest regret.

Sensitivity to time underscores the reality that many unfortunate and even tragic events become funny with the passage of time. I had a friend who was in a terrible hit and run accident, and the two men who were witnesses to the accident jumped into their vehicles to chase the man who hit her. They left her lying in the street. Fortunately, she was okay. I visited her in the hospital later that day and she was quite shaken and did not want to talk about what happened. When I approached the door to her hospital room the following day, however, I heard her tell her story to one of the nurses. They were crying from laughing so hard. "So there I am, bleeding and bruised, lying in the street, after being thrown from my mangled car. These two nimrods are so upset by what they just saw, and boiling over in some kind of vicarious-vengeful rage, that they *both* get into their cars to chase the

73

guy, and *leave me there all by my f@#$ing self!*" The difference between tragedy and comedy was 24 hours.

Find the Humor in Adversity

Why do some people choke and some do not? Just before a tennis tournament or an important business call, successful people control stress and shut out distraction. They have complete focus and concentrate fully. They don't even consider the possibility of failure. They reach a tranquil state which calms down the heart and brain functions. Their beliefs and attitudes affect performance outcome.

Likewise, changing your attitude changes your feelings, which alters your performance and gives you a new perspective. Take what has happened to you and decide to change it. Look at it from a different angle. Make your most embarrassing moment into your funniest story. What caused the change? You. The events are the same. Change your perception of the events and change your physiological response to them. Change your memory and improve your health.

As a weekly exercise, I suggest you recall one event from the prior week that was not so funny at the time, and make it funny. Tell the story to someone and use whatever language, pauses, inflection, and gestures are necessary to make someone laugh. You will be altering your own memory of the event, honing your creativity, entertaining yourself, and entertaining someone else. Now that's a win/win.

Feed Your Funny Bone

Another weekly exercise I highly recommend is a stroll through the comedy section at your local video store. Begin at the A's and just read the titles and look at the covers. I guarantee you will not be able to keep a straight face even up to the M's. Make a list of your favorites and the ones you'd like to see and make a point of renting one each week. You might like to go to the stand-up comedy section and do the same. The point is to experience some good ole' comedy on a regular basis.

In addition, are there any authors you find particularly funny? Do you like the comics? Do you like cartoons (I recommend some classic Bugs Bunny and Road Runner compilations)? In short, feed your funny bone. Remember, laughter actually improves your disposition and your health. The healthier you are inside, the healthier you will be outside.

Intuition

Thinkers from theologians to physicists have been trying to determine the exact nature and origin of intuition for hundreds of years at least, and they have yet to reach a consensus. We all seem to know, perhaps *intuitively*, what we refer to when we speak of intuition. However, when we try to discuss details, the topic gets fuzzy. Whether intuition is really God talking to us, our bodies picking up unseen signals around us, or our minds tapping into the universal consciousness, one thing is clear: We all have experienced moments when our intuition has helped us. And when you experience something that helps your performance in life, you should want to duplicate that type of experience as often as possible.

The history of the intuition debate is beyond the scope of this book and will be covered in my next book. For the purpose of this discussion, there are just five truths you need to know. I call them truths because they are probably the only aspects of intuition that there is consensus on. They are only difficult to believe if you don't want to believe they are true.

1. Women don't have more of it than men.

2. Everybody has it and can further develop it.

3. It is not otherworldly or supernatural.

4. It is never wrong.

5. It can help improve your effectiveness and efficiency in every aspect of your life.

If any of these five is a tough sell, you have not been cultivating your intuition. Intuition, like listening, is about attending to signals. To maximize your listening, you want to pay attention to what is said and what is not said: to all of the signals related to a message. Likewise, to optimize your intuition you want to develop your skill at paying attention to what your body is telling you. In other words, intuition is about listening to yourself. This means you need to learn to be quiet and still, a state many of us won't reach until death.

The reason most of us ignore our intuition is that we are so accustomed to basing our decisions on real things, such as what we can see and what we can hear. My question is: In what way are those things more real than what you feel? How often do you think you have heard and understood someone, only to find out that you haven't? So you'll work on your listening skills to decrease those occurrences, right? Well how many times have you had a gut feeling about something and discovered that your gut feeling was wrong? Has your gut feeling ever been wrong?

Yeah, But I have those gut feelings about really important things ...maybe once a month-tops ...and the feeling is pretty extreme.

Yes you do have those "extreme" experiences. And you have less obvious ones every day in between, as well; you're just not listening. And when you are, you aren't thinking about it because it is perfectly natural to go along with your feelings and not think about it. Those extreme moments probably occur because you weren't listening to the more subtle messages your body was sending you, so it had to do something drastic to get your attention.

For most of us raised in the West, making decisions based on things like feelings is not easy. We are a materialistic culture in every sense of the word. We worship the material; what we can touch and quantify and manipulate. This is not a bad thing. But as a consequence of our "civilized" ways, we have lost contact with one of the most primitive parts of ourselves. That part was responsible for our decision-making long before we could write impeccably polished prose describing our line of reasoning. In fact, reasoning is precisely the act that can lead us astray.

"It is ironic that academic psychology, which has tried to model itself after the physical sciences, dismisses intuition except as unconscious reasoning or inference, while physical scientists are much readier to acknowledge intuition as a process that is fundamentally different from, and superior to, reason, in discovering truth"(Arthur Deikman, M..D., in Inner Knowing).

So reasoning is a problem?

Yes and no. When I say that your intuition is never wrong, I mean it. But that's not the whole story. What your intuition is giving you is actually the *answer* to a question that you may not have asked yet (or don't think you were planning to ask). The actual cue that you get in your body, whether it is a physical one (a gut feeling), a mental one (eureka!), or an emotional one (I immediately disliked her when I met her and I couldn't tell you why), is always valid. However, when you begin to interpret it, *when you have to try to figure out what question it is answering*, you can make a mistake. If your reasoning about your intuition is faulty it will create a faulty response/reaction. The intuition itself, as Deikman says, is superior to reason.

You respond to your intuition far more often than you may realize. These instances go undetected by your conscious mind because your reaction occurs immediately following your cue. If you were to put many of these moments back-to-back, you might say that you were "in the zone." The zone is a period of time when you are doing everything you are supposed to be doing, the way you are supposed to be doing it. You are not conscious of the choices you make; you just make them effortlessly and your performance is at its peak. In fact, some people describe it as a *peak moment.* "I was perfect. I couldn't have handled it better if I tried." Does that sound familiar? That is one of the results of respecting your intuition.

How do I improve my use of my intuition?
Self-Discovery #5b-Intuition

The process of improving your use of your intuition involves taking some time to get acquainted with it. You see, every person's intuition is unique, which is why I cannot possibly interpret the answers *you* are getting.

Therefore, your first step is *to choose to attend to your intuition.* For the next couple of days, record the moments when you are having a hunch, a gut feeling, or an aha! I prefer the use of a microcassette recorder to trying to write everything down because I can never write fast enough and invariably lose potentially important information. Any time you do something without knowing why, record that moment as soon as you realize it occurred. Intuition is a tool just like the brain. And just like the brain, it gets better and stronger with use. The more conscious you are of the signals you get, the louder they will seem to become for you.

This exercise brings an unconscious moment to the consciousness and some people find it a bit unnerving. It is analogous to what happens when you are deciding whether to purchase a new car and you suddenly begin to see the car everywhere you go. In other words, the more you put your attention on your intuition, the more you will notice its presence.

Don't begin to record until you have responded

When doing this exercise, some people are quickly faced with what appears to be the realization that their intuition isn't working for their benefit. This occurs when you become so aware of your intuitive moments that you begin to think about what they might mean rather than just responding naturally. When you try to reason, you introduce the possibility of an error in your interpretation of your cue. If you were to record before you responded, you would risk producing a faulty response.

What are you trying to accomplish by taking notes?

Your intuition is a bit like your dreams in that it uses a system of symbols that is unique to you. This is why only you can interpret your dreams accurately. For instance, suppose I have a recurring dream about my teeth falling out. The image of losing your teeth is nothing new in the dream interpretation world. However, what it means to me (anxiety about an upcoming seminar, perhaps) could be different from what it means to you.

Similarly, I might get butterflies in my stomach when I am anticipating something that is good, while you might get them when you are anticipating something bad. What matters is that you take note of the kinds of signals you get and what you think they mean based on

77

how you reacted. Do you get images, words, symbols, colors, or physical manifestations such as "the willies?" How does your intuition work?

At the end of a week, listen to your recordings and refresh your memory about the kinds of intuitive feelings or thoughts you had, what the context seemed to be, and what the outcome was. The most interesting occurrences are usually the ones where your intuition didn't seem to work; where you made a conscious decision that was an error. This is proof positive that reasoning is not as effective as intuition.

Intuition by design

Once you are a bit acquainted with your intuition, when you try to call it to your aid you are more likely to recognize it. The next time you need an answer to a question, write the question down. This first step is not as easy as it sounds because your wording is of the utmost importance. If, for instance, you want to know whether you should accept a position you were offered or remain at your current job, you need to be as specific as possible. Your question should read, "Should I stay at X corporation in my present position as VP of Marketing or should I accept the offer of Y.com as their Master of Mischief?" The phrasing "Should I take the job at Y.com?" will not be as effective because there may be many job openings at Y.com. You will get the answer to the question you asked, so be sure to ask the right question. And where do you think this answer comes from? Some mystical place far above you? No. Actually, it comes from below—in your gut. Just like Dorothy in *The Wizard of Oz*, you have the power and the answers. You just have to learn how to use them.

After you have worded your question, read it a dozen times, trying to focus on just the words you are reading, then stop. Immediately begin to record the images and symbols and colors that come to mind and the feelings you are having, both emotionally (I'm sad) and physically (my heart is racing and I am getting a stomachache). Do not, I repeat, *do not* interpret the feelings and images, just make note of them. Do this for about a minute. Some people prefer keeping their eyes opened, some like to close their eyes.

After you have recorded the cues you have received, review them. Without interpreting them too much, you should be able to tell whether the answer to your question appears to be positive or negative. If you are unsure, look at each item on your list and create a brief sentence about what it means to you. This is the interpretation part: the opportunity for error. But if you don't try too hard to interpret each item—if you just let your natural response come to the forefront of your thoughts—you will not steer yourself in the wrong direction.

Someone in one of my seminars did this exercise for the first time and this is what happened. He is an investment advisor for a major brokerage firm and his three years of hard work and long hours were finally beginning to pay off. He was questioning if he should pursue a referral that would have 1) taken him away from his family for a very important weekend and 2) cost him two thousand dollars, but could 3) bring him a $10 million account (and would be his largest, single account), with the possibility of many more referrals.

He did this exercise and came up with, among other things, a very cold feeling, the image of a frozen lake where he used to play ice hockey as a child (there were no people on it but there were hockey sticks and goal nets), and an image of the Porsche he was wanted to buy (he chose a less expensive family car instead because he realized a sports car wasn't a very good idea for him at that time). His list of items seemed random and meaningless to him at first.

Upon reviewing the list, however, he immediately knew that the answer to his question was no. He doesn't like feeling cold, so that item was a negative for him. The frozen lake image, as he explained it, meant "what good is the lake and all of the equipment without the people—there's something crucial missing." He knew that he made the right decision by not purchasing the Porsche, so he figured this question was somehow analogous.

He later discovered that the $10 million was in the account of a person who is a citizen and resident of Canada, and that under his company's rules, he could not get the money. Perhaps the expensive trip would have produced a couple of referrals, but he would have missed his family event, and that should have been his priority (kind of like the rationale behind his Porsche decision).

Getting to Know You

The most effective decision-makers are those who are hardly aware that they have made decisions. They follow their intuition and don't question, obsess, or overanalyze. When you ask them why they have taken a certain route (figuratively or otherwise), they can't even tell you why. Instead, they say something like "because I knew I was supposed to" or, "It just felt right." They have learned to trust their intuition because they have experienced the reality that it will serve them well.

Fortunately, we can all get to that point. All it takes is attention, patience, and the all-important belief that you can always trust your intuition to steer you in the right direction.

Creative Thinking

Why discuss creative thinking? In my experience, the more agile, flexible, and creative you are, the easier it is for you to achieve win/win outcomes in your communications. Just as there are exercises you need to do to increase the flexibility of your body, there are ways to exercise your mind to increase its flexibility. Those exercises involve the development of a range of ways of thinking and responding so you are equipped to deal with whatever situations you encounter.

Creative thinking enables you to transform your communication breakdowns into communication break*throughs*. It helps you to strengthen your communication muscles and improve your reflexes and your timing. Complete communicators see beyond what they look at and hear more than just what is being said. They choose toned words and use meaningful body language. And they are able to build strong and lasting relationships because they are flexible in their thinking and their communicating. They have embraced the value of expanding their mind and their responses beyond the realm of the ordinary.

Creative Thinking Defined

Have you heard the one about how we humans use 10 percent of our brains' capacity? It was just a rumor. As it turns out, the figure is more in the neighborhood of *less than one percent*. Now, given that measly number, you'd think that we would be doing everything in our power to up that figure to, maybe, a whopping three or four percent. Wrong again. It seems that, without intervention, our brains will take the path of least resistance, and opt for as little work as possible. As Edward de Bono notes in his *de Bono's Thinking Course*,

The main purpose of thinking is to abolish thinking. The mind works to make sense out of confusion and uncertainty. The mind works to recognize familiar patterns in the outside world. As soon as such a pattern is recognized the mind switches into it and follows along—further thinking is unnecessary (35).

This does not bode well for us, but that doesn't mean we can't do anything about it. If the main purpose of thinking is to abolish thinking by sticking to familiar patterns, I'm going to define the main purpose of creative thinking as *to produce thinking by constantly trying new patterns.*

Change Your Hat, Change Your Thinking

In Edward de Bono's international bestseller, *Six Thinking Hats*, he proposes a system for helping individuals and groups think in a more productive and creative way. The six hats are different colors, and each represents a different way to think:

White=objective and neutral

80

Red=emotional

Black=cautious

Yellow=positive

Green=creative

Blue=organizational

De Bono did not create this system as another way of categorizing people and putting them in boxes. He is clear that his purpose is not to provide yet another way of labeling people. That is not my purpose either.

The purpose is to embrace that we all wear these hats at different times. True, we each tend to favor a particular hat or two. However, the pure act of reminding us that there are different ways of thinking and representing them in such a simple and useful fashion (colored hats), makes it easy to switch hats and change your thinking. When you are familiar with the different ways of thinking and are comfortable switching among them, you can communicate more effectively with more people because of your ability to see alternatives. Furthermore, when you understand where someone else is coming from (e.g., he's got his red hat on; watch out, the language coming at you could be hazardous to your health), you can better predict their behavior and prepare a response that has a good chance of being heard.

Another aspect of this system that makes it so useful is that you don't have to teach it to everyone you know in order for it to immensely improve your thinking and your relationships. Again, I emphasize the need for self-knowledge first.

Self-Discovery Exercise #5c-Creative Thinking

You can use the buddy system accompanied by a microcassette recorder to help you with this self-discovery. The purpose here is to determine your dominant style when you are dealing either with a new idea or one that could become a problem. I suggest you tape yourself for a week at random times and when you are having important conversations. The recordings will give you an idea of the way you think, in general. Also, ask your buddy to pay attention to how you approach issues the two of you discuss.

When you are speaking to another person—any person—you will probably alter what you say or how you say it in an attempt to get the desired response from the other person. You may not even be aware that you do this. Therefore, your buddy's feedback, as well as the conversations you record, might not accurately reflect the way you think. Getting around this potential problem is easy: do your thinking out loud for a week and record your mind's meanderings. When you are not speaking with an audience in mind you won't alter your words or tone. When you play back the tapes you are sure to discover the dominant way you think, just from noting your choice of words.

This exercise will help you determine, if you didn't already know, how you think, how those thoughts gets translated into the words you choose, and where all of this is getting you. Review the segments of recorded conversations. What kinds of responses do you get from listeners? Can you tell, from your recordings, how much interest your listeners have for your ideas? What is the tone of their responses? What is the length (e.g., do you get a lot of one word answers?) Do they respond with questions of their own that further develop topics you have introduced?

After you have reviewed the recordings of your conversations, listen to the recordings of your thinking aloud. Is there any difference?

Regardless of whether you deem your thinking pattern successful, the best way to expand your mental faculties is to exercise them. When you have a distinct pattern with which you handle most situations, you are in effect on autopilot. And when you are on autopilot, your brain is working as little as possible. Like any muscle or any skill you have, the less you use it, the less it gets developed.

Creative Thinking in Action

Did you know that on an unconscious level we *calibrate* the reactions of others and they do the same to us? Calibration refers to noticing the patterns of others and responding in a way that best utilizes that knowledge. For example, if you were a professional card player and played for hour after hour, you would begin to notice the patterns of others within the card-playing context. Can you imagine playing cards with someone and noticing that every time they were bluffing they pulled their chair a little closer to the table? Or maybe they cleared their throat before they bet when they had a great hand.

We all leak signals like these every day. Those of us who pay attention to the signals of others can calibrate the reactions of others based on how they usually react. If you pay attention to all signals you can better gauge where you are in any communication situation. Creative thinking helps you to remember not to keep doing what you've always done. There's a famous, albeit overused, quote in motivational circles that is true for everyone. "If you always do what you've always done, you'll always get what you've always gotten."

Getting Off Autopilot

"When we actually set out to find alternatives it is not all that difficult to find some.... The real difficulty is to set out to look for alternatives in the first place (de Bono, Thinking Course 25).

This quote describes the paradox of creative thinking. When we set out to change our thinking, we are usually successful. The actual changing of the thinking isn't difficult; *recognizing that you need to change it is the real problem.*

The best way around this dilemma is to create a new pattern: one that is characterized by constant change. Get into the habit of looking anywhere and everywhere for the solutions to your problems or the generation of new ideas. In fact, go further than that. Tomorrow, when you begin your day, make the choice to do everything differently. Have a salad for breakfast, take a route to work that begins and ends with the same street, but has all new ones in between, and when you get to work, question all of the decisions you make and look for alternatives. Drive home via yet another different route. Have something completely new for dinner. Change everything about your day except where you put your keys (there's creativity, and then there's insanity). You may be far more exhausted than usual at the end of the day, but that's simply because you were working harder.

Thinking and creativity are organic and expansive processes that use energy. Once you become more creative in your thinking, you open the channels to alter all other areas of your life because they are all intimately connected to thinking. Remember, the process goes like this: Your thoughts affect the words you choose, and the words you choose affect your emotions, your relationships, and even your health.

Exercises similar to this are recommended for mature adults who are concerned about what they think is the deterioration of their memories. This is based on the common misconception that our memory gets worse as we age. The reality is that memory, again, just like a muscle, seems to atrophy due to lack of use. Stimulation, use, is the way to maintain it.

Have you ever had the experience when you were driving to work or some other place that you frequent and you cannot remember how you got there? Yes, you drove and you were in your car and you know what route you took. After all, it was the route you always take. But you don't recall actually doing it. That's because you were on autopilot. Tomorrow morning, decide to take yourself off autopilot. I promise you, you'll remember your trip to work.

Techniques for Thinking Outside the Box

Your mind wants all new information to fit into boxes (patterns) that already exist in your unique brain. If new information does not fit exactly, your mind will make it fit so that a new box does not have to be created. Your mind does not like uncertainty, so it will eliminate it, even if that means changing the input a bit. It will treat new information as if it really matches the existing patterns in the absence of alternatives. This is why you have to make a conscious choice to become a creative thinker and communicator and then commit to practicing your new craft. Your mind has a different agenda. In order to begin to think outside of the mental boxes you have created for yourself, I recommend you increase the time you spend on the following activities: playing, daydreaming, artistic expression, sports, and listening.

Playing

Perhaps the easiest way to begin to see the world differently is through something you were an expert at long before you perfected your sense of logic—**playing**. Go into any fourth grade classroom and you'll find a bunch of youngsters who have no sense of fear or ego when it comes to problem solving. They ask all kinds of questions; whether any are "stupid" questions is not an issue. Everything is a game to them. The world is a source of wonder. When they want to figure something out, they'll try anything and won't stop when something doesn't work.

Keep in mind that having fun is first an attitude, then a process.
—*Jordan Ayan, Aha! 10 Ways to Free Your Creative Spirit and Find Your Great Ideas, 128).*

If you approach any situation expecting it to be fun, you will find ways to make it fun and you will free yourself from the shackles of the serious problem-solving behavior you have become so good at. The notion of play somehow gives us permission to go back to the days of trial and error without judgment. It also permits us to engage in behavior *just because it is fun*. I'm talking about no apologies, no objectives, no reasoning—just plain fun.

When you are looking for an answer or an idea in a specific place, you are sure to find *something*. But when you are not looking for an answer in a specific place, when you are receptive to all that is around you and are not quick to judge its value or usefulness, you are more likely to see possible answers all around you.

Daydreaming

Another way to expand your mind is by **daydreaming**. Creative thinkers seize every opportunity to produce their own little mental movies and music videos about how life could be. Creative thinkers don't adjust their daydreams to conform to reality. Instead, they embrace the chance to conjure up scenarios that are completely outrageous. It is precisely this ability to release all of your inner fairy tales that will help you see alternatives to problems and create new and exciting ideas. Thinking how you always thought will just produce more of the same ole' thoughts. You have to step outside of the system you unconsciously have created for yourself.

Artistic Expression

Perhaps the most obvious way to increase your creativity is to **increase your artistic expression**. This is particularly important if you do not see yourself as an artistic person and you do not normally produce anything with your hands. I should know, because I can safely say that I am the least artistic person I know.

However, in an attempt to bolster my creative thinking, a couple of months ago I took up watercolors and pastels (I'd recommend neither if you have a tendency toward making a mess. If you do, I suggest colored pencils or maybe photography). I spent the first month learning about my new materials by wrecking several pads of paper (the water part of watercolors must be managed carefully, I discovered) and staining my furniture and carpet (did you know that a vacuum cleaner can remove most colors of pastels if you don't try to wash them out first?).

Now, I won't claim to be any good at either of my new endeavors, but there is a discernible change in my thinking as a result of trying my hand at them. First of all, because I tried them in the privacy of my own home, I felt no pressure to do anything a particular way or to produce something that looked like even an attempt at art. There's nothing like a roomful of people to quash every creative tendency you might have had. Because I was not worried about being judged incompetent, I let my creative self run wild and discovered that I am capable of more than I imagined. Don't get me wrong, my stuff wasn't award winning. But it was better than I expected, and with practice I have improved immensely.

As a result of my foray into the fine arts, I have also found that I see things differently. I notice things in a different way. The qualities of colors and textures around me are something I attend to for the first time. I have spent a considerable amount of time (relatively speaking—for me) blending, mixing, diluting, and smudging. I have observed as a seemingly insignificant amount of water, or a slight increase in the pressure of a hand or a brush, can completely alter the look of a color or a line. It can alter the statement that color or line makes. I started to think of the people around me as those pastels and watercolors. I pondered how they could change in one direction or

85

another, based on the influence of an outside source. I linked persuasion to pastels—now that's creative.

I realized that I was developing a different kind of intelligence (for more on the theory of multiple intelligences, see Howard Gardner's *Frames of Mind: The Theory of Multiple Intelligences*): one that involves aesthetic appreciation rather than a concentration on words and logic. I became much more comfortable thinking in images rather than just words, and my intuition was given that new form of expression as well. I was becoming a better thinker because I was becoming more versatile.

Sports

Involvement in **sports** tends to create a similar phenomenon, particularly for people who are not ordinarily physically active. When you develop your kinesthetic intelligence, you become aware of muscles you didn't know you had by learning movements you have never tried before.

I was always considered a good athlete, you know, for a girl. Every sport I tried was easy for me. I got up on water skis the first time, and dropped a ski without incident. I was always one of the first people chosen for the baseball teams and the guys would even back up when I got up to bat. Snow skiing, ice skating, tennis—they were all a cinch. Then I met my match.

How difficult could golf really be, I asked myself. After all, it's played mostly by out of shape guys. The first time I picked up a golf club (a driver) and tried to hit a ball, all I could think about was how easy it was going to be. Then reality hit me. The physics of it all seemed a bit dangerous when I realized that if I actually took a serious swing and my form and grip were off, the club could very well slam into the ground and I could break my arms. I couldn't conceive of the club just grazing the ground. I felt like a fool, I looked like a fool, but after a couple dozen tries, I actually hit the ball.

Now I must confess that I do not like golf. I took it up because everyone at the business meetings I went to played and talked incessantly about the game, their scores, and everyone else's scores. I took some private lessons with a pro with a very simple goal in mind: not to embarrass myself in front of clients and colleagues on the golf course. My instructor was great; he gave me a few pointers that really helped. Things like: shut up, move quickly, and learn how to drive the ball straight for 100 yards. Sounded reasonable to me—at least the shut up and move quickly part.

Fortunately, there is a two-pronged happy ending to this story:

1. Learning how to play golf has given me new metaphors—new ways of approaching life. For instance, the short game—put-

ting—is so important, yet most people practice driving far more. Putting is about details, polish, and patience. It is about comparatively tiny movements that have the ability to put the ball in the hole. Is there anything in your life that's like putting?

2. Following the rules (shut up, move quickly, learn to drive ball 100 yards in a straight line) might have actually helped my career (read: not destroyed it). At a very fancy club (i.e., totally intimidating) in Short Hills, New Jersey, I was in something they called a shotgun start scramble formation (I think). Anyway, I was in the first cart with the "big boss" and was told that hole #5 was sponsored by someone and the person closest to the pin won some kind of prize. Although I was itching to ask what "closest to the pin" meant, I remembered trusty Rule #1, which instructed me to shut up. I also wanted to inquire about shotguns and scrambles but thought silence was a better idea. Instead, I enlisted Rule #3, and just hit the ball. 100 yards. Straight. The hole was 105 yards. I win. The boss has newfound respect for me (if he only knew ....).

Listening

Finally, I am a firm believer that developing your **listening** skills not only bolsters your memory, but is also a requirement for developing creative thinking. Synesthesia is a fancy word for your mental ability to use all your senses. "When you are listening, keep your other senses, especially sight, actively involved. The more you can link your senses, the better your hearing, attention, understanding and general learning will be" (Buzan, *Make the Most of Your Mind*, 71).

For instance, the next time you drive to a new place, pay attention to the road, yes, but also roll the windows down and smell your trip. Look past the road and notice the neighborhood. Listen with your ears to the sounds of your travels. Listen also to your intuition and note what kinds of signals you are getting. As a result of involving all of your senses in your trip, you are more likely to recall the details of the travel as well as the new destination. If you needed a map or written directions for your first trip, you will probably be able to do without them thereafter. When you learn to listen—really listen—you will hear what you need to hear rather than what you choose to hear.

Versatility

Versatility of mind is a hallmark of creative thinking. Exploring your various intelligences and ways of thinking is a great way to increase the versatility of your mind. So although you can identify your dominant way of processing information (i.e., visual, auditory, or kinesthetic), developing your skill at the other two modes, or practicing changing Thinking Hats, is a valuable strategy to nurture your creative thinking ability.

Another kind of versatility comes from the knowledge of a variety of different fields of endeavor. In order to broaden your general knowledge, learn about a topic you have an interest in but that you have never pursued. Better yet, learn about a topic you have no interest in and really test your ability to soak up new information.

Whenever I suggest this, someone invariably comments that "you can only know so much." Another fallacy. As Tony Buzan notes in *Make the Most of Your Mind*, "even if the brain were fed ten new bits of information every second for its entire life, it would be nowhere near full" (39). Don't worry about the capacity of your brain. Each time you learn something new you create new connections in your brain to existing information and you strengthen the existing information (your long-term memory).

Creative Thinking and Persuasion

Creativity is usually greeted with attention and appreciation, which are two desirable factors in any situation involving persuasion. Someone is more likely to listen to you (and then be influenced by you) if what you are telling them and the way you are communicating is not what they would expect. This is often the basis for humor. I'll end this section with an anecdote that sums up the connection between creative thinking and persuasion.

My friend Angie is one of the most creative salespeople and communicators I know. Many years ago, we were involved with a talented gentleman who enlisted our aid to sell his products. Unfortunately, time after time, we found it difficult to get the answers we needed from him in order to make good business decisions. Angie proposed we have a festive and formal group dinner in his honor, and present him with an award. We thanked him for his immense talent, boundless energy, and groundbreaking ideas. Then, we unveiled a beautiful plaque with his name engraved at the bottom. The plaque had a pair of tap shoes on a velvet background. The inscription said: "To xxxx, The Tap Dance Kid." This was a flawlessly executed combination of creativity and knowing your audience. Our guest of honor laughed uproariously and acknowledged his part in making our work difficult. He promised to do better in the future. Sold!

Summary
- Your humor, you intuition, and your creative thinking are all aspects of your internal life that affect your external life. They affect your confidence, your body language, and your capacity for problem solving.

- Getting in touch with who you are and what is going on inside your heart and head—learning how to communicate with your self—helps hone your awareness of how you communicate with others. When you have mastered how you communicate, it is easier to then examine and decode what others want and need in communication.
- Fortunately, humor, intuition, and creative thinking are all parts of your self that can be improved. With some attention and intention, your invisibles will help you become a better, more successful communicator.

CHAPTER SEVEN

The Art of Cross Addressing

Gender issues have been a national obsession here in America for about a decade. After all of the research, the trials, the longitudinal studies, and the cross cultural studies, it seems that everyone from teachers to doctors to financial advisors has come to the same startling conclusion: men and women are different. Some of the differences that have received a lot of airtime in the mainstream media and entered everyday conversations from boardrooms to schoolrooms to operating rooms, are:

- our learning styles

- the way we think

- the way we approach romantic relationships

- how we make decisions

- how we communicate

- how we prefer to socialize

- how we deal with our emotions

Though these differences do receive a lot of publicity, not all of the "experts" agree that men and women are as dramatically different as we are alleged to be. For my purpose here, however, I am not assuming that I know what the real truth is. What I do know, is that most people in America have come to believe that men and women are different in the ways listed above and many others. The truth of this conventional wisdom is not the subject of my discussion. Men and women clearly need to learn how to better relate with each other. Using the conventional wisdom is the path I have chosen.

Choosing that path makes it necessary for me to offer a caveat: Gender differences is one of those topics where a little knowledge is a dangerous thing. I am referring to the tendency to stereotype, generalize, and excuse people for their behavior because, "boys will be boys," or "it's a woman thing." I request that when you read this chapter you keep in mind that I am describing, in a general way, how men and women *tend* to behave. In fact, I use the word *tend* quite frequently to remind you that these are generalizations. There are plenty of exceptions. In fact, I am an exception in several ways, and you may find the same is true for you and some people you know. My purpose here is to help you relate with both sexes by presenting their differences—not to give you another reason to lump all women together as (insert your favorite stereotype) or all men as (ditto).

In fact, I think the best way to begin this discussion is to dispel some common myths. Here's a short quiz I begin many of my seminars with. It has been adapted from Lillian Glass' book *He Says, She Says*, which influenced my thinking about gender more than any other book. Much of this chapter is based on Glass' findings.

True or False

1. Women are more intuitive than men. They have a sixth sense, typically called "women's intuition."
2. Women are talkers. They talk much more than men do in group conversations.
3. Men are more outwardly open. They use more eye contact and exhibit more friendliness when meeting someone new.
4. Men ask more questions than women.
5. Women tend to touch others more often than men.

Now let's see how you did. . .

1. False. Recall the discussion about intuition in Chapter Five. As Glass says, though women may pay greater attention to detail, they do not possess intuition in any greater quantity than men. According to world-renowned anthropologist Ashley Montague, women have a greater sensitivity and acuity for color. Linguist Robin Lakoff, in her classic book, *Language and Woman's Place*, concurs and explains that women tend to use finer descriptions of color. For instance, they will use words like bone, persimmon, and ebony. (Women—ask any man you know what primary colors cornflower and periwinkle are closest to. Men—do you know?)

    This attention to detail might make women seem more intuitive, but the reality is more like they just tend to notice characteristics that men tend to miss, such as a person's body language, vocal tones, and facial expressions. In addition, women are oftentimes better at perceiving a person's mood and emotional state, which makes them appear to be more intuitive. Women simply attend to different details than men do. Women tend to focus on emotions and relationships, while men tend to focus on facts and projects.

2. False. Contrary to the popular stereotype, it is men who talk more. In fact, men far out talk women in mixed-sex conversation.

3. False. Numerous studies show that it is women who maintain more eye contact and facial pleasantries. Furthermore, in positive interactions, women increase eye contact while men decrease eye contact. Women exhibit more friendly behavior such as smiles, facial pleasantries, and head nods than men do, especially when meeting someone new. Even though women were found to smile 93 percent of the time, only 67 percent of their smiles were returned by men.

4. False. Just as women raise more topics of conversation than men do, they also ask more questions. Questions posing functions to facilitate the conversation.

5. False. Men tend to touch more than women do. According to several research studies, women are more likely to be physically touched by men, who tend to guide women through doors, assist them with their coats, and help them into cars. Men also touch one another (e.g., backslaps, handshakes, high-fives) more than women touch one another.

Nature or Nurture

The most unnerving question regarding gender differences is whether they are present at birth (innate) or whether they are acquired. I don't know the answer to the question. I'd imagine the correct answer is not one or the other, but rather a blend. My favorite way of explaining the nature/nurture debate is a story I have come to call *I Never Played Third Base*, or, *Why Women and Men Need to be Managed Differently.*

Over the years, time and again, men have told me of their frustrations with managing women. I thought about this in the context of other life experiences. I thought about the closest man to me, my brother, who is two years younger than I. His first corporate experience, as I like to call it, took place at the age of seven, when he played baseball.

He learned that the goal was to win—to beat the competition.

He learned that the coach was the boss, and he got used to being told what to do by the coach, and doing just that.

He learned that the coach's son got to pitch.

He learned that the best player started even if he missed practice.

He learned to take criticism. Sometimes it was very, very harsh.

He learned to sit next to the coach on the bench and stroke him rather than sulk.

He learned that you could strike out twice and then be a hero on your third attempt.

He learned about instruction and practice.

He learned teamwork. (Even if Michael Jordan scored 56 points, he wasn't happy if his team didn't win.)

He learned locker room behavior, including how to give and receive criticism and praise, and all of the language, noises, and physical movement that accompanied that behavior.

Years later, my brother found that all of the same rules still existed. His path to and through the corporate world went swimmingly. He had very few surprises.

Meanwhile, I was not even encouraged to participate in sports outside of the required physical education class (although I did, with the guys in the neighborhood, and luckily I was gifted athletically). My locker room memories from gym class were of each person being locked in a private stall where the goal was to not make any sounds. I recall girls saying only nice things and being very modest and very respectful of the privacy of others. I don't recall getting slapped on the back, or any other part of my body, for that matter, and I certainly didn't engage in anything remotely resembling "trash talk." On the contrary, I recall other girls telling me how great I was on the field or court, even when my performance was pitiful. And while on the field, I saw plenty of girls manipulate their way out of participating by crying or suddenly not feeling well. I doubt that kind of behavior was acceptable in the boys' class.

As girls, we were told how pretty and sweet we were. In school, we learned about Ultimate Justice: if you spelled all ten words correctly on a test, you got a 100. Simple as that. We learned to expect justice and for the world to be fair.

Our first competition was at twelve or thirteen, and we all competed for the same thing—a boy. We learned to see each other as the threat and the competition. Sadly, this is still going on.

Cross Gender Communication-Frustration

Perhaps it is as a result of being taught about performance on a team at an early age, that when you tell a man in your office that something he did is not up to par, he grumbles and then does it over. Meanwhile, when you tell a woman her performance is not up to par, she thinks she is a bad person and that you hate her.

The lessons we all learned about competition as children affect how we behave as adults. Because women view each other as competition, and are constantly on the lookout for whom their competition is, it is important for men to not show favorites among the women. This kind of environment can quickly become an adversarial one, with the women trying to beat each other rather than their real business opponents. In order to get along in a group that has women in it, the most important thing to remember is that women do not require *special* treatment—they require *fair* treatment. And fair treatment means not showing favorites.

Some say men are, by nature, selfish, aggressive creatures whose mission in life is to conquer. The same people usually say women are, by nature, nurturing and compassionate, and their mission in life is to optimize the happiness of others. Go to any playground and watch the boys and the girls. I'm fairly certain you'll find that their mannerisms, the tones of their voices, their language (both verbal and nonverbal) and the way they deal with conflict when they play, is different. Whether we condition those differences into them is hardly the point for those of us who are now adults and have to coexist at home and in the workplace.

One of my favorite stories about gender differences is about a woman who is the mother of a four year old boy. Though she is a first-time mother, she has read all of the books on child development and she knows that children begin to speak (in words) at about age two. Her child has never even tried to utter a word. She tells her mother of her concern and confides in several of the neighborhood mothers. She eventually takes him to a speech pathologist, who can find nothing wrong with his vocal apparatus. Then one day, he blurts out, "Mom, the toast is burned!" She hugs him and kisses him and says, "Sweetie, why has it taken you so long to talk?" After a pause, the boy responds, "Up until now, things have been okay."

Participants in my seminars often tell me of their frustration over how men and women became so different, just how different they really are, and, above all, *whose way is better*! My response is always the same—it doesn't matter. What matters is that we are here, and now we have to learn to deal with our differences, without judgment.

94

Cross Addressing, or, Bridging the Gender Gap

The secret to bridging the gap between you and anyone, is to let the other person lead the dance. Your starting point, no matter what your topic of conversation is or what your motivation is, should always be the other person. So if you are a man speaking to a woman, you may need to cross address. Likewise for a woman speaking to a man. I say "may" because some women possess more of the stereotypical male characteristics than the female ones, and the same is true for some men. These people generally know who they are. A girlfriend of mine calls herself the *unfemale*. She says she was always keenly aware of the differences between men and women because *people constantly tell her that she doesn't act like a typical woman.*

Cross addressing means simply that you present yourself, including your words, your tone, and your body language, in a way that is similar to the person to whom you are speaking. Remember that we like people who are like us. The more similar you are to your audience, the more comfortable they will be. And when people are comfortable, they are receptive to your message.

The Gap

The gender gap is a result of differences in the ways we communicate, process information, and then react to it. Within the general topic of communication are: the words we use, the way we sound, the way we listen, and the way we look. Here are a couple of tips...

What You Say

- Men tend to give a lot of commands (e.g., "Get me a beer"). In contrast, women use fewer command terms and opt for the request (e.g., "Honey, would you be kind enough to get me a beer?"). The mistake is to infer that he wants the beer more than she does. He might, but we don't know that from what he said, because that's just his way of speaking. So if you are a woman speaking to a man, saying "Let's get started" is fine, but if you're a man speaking to a woman, she might find you a bit abrupt. Remember who your audience is, and *cross address*, if necessary.
- Men use fewer descriptive terms and intensifiers than women use. (Guess who said, "That's a really, really great suit; the color is soooooo beautiful. Then guess who said, "Nice suit.") If you are a man, *cross addressing* would include using more descriptive terms and intensifiers.
- Men and women use different kinds of quantifiers. Men favor definitive terms such as *always, all, never,* and *none*, while women prefer the less definitive terms such as *kind of* and *a*

bit. Men think that women are less certain when their termi-
nology is not definitive. Meanwhile, women think that men are
trying to bully them or hard sell them when they use definitive
terms. If you are a woman *cross addressing*, remember that
your listener wants to hear terms that reflect certainty.

- The commands that men give do not require any further
explanation (e.g., Get me a beer). Meanwhile, the requests of
women are often followed, or preceded, by an explanation
(e.g., Honey, would you be kind enough to get me a beer; I'm
soooooo thirsty). If you are a man, *cross addressing* might
include what you think is unnecessary (of course I'm thirsty,
why else would I ask for a beer), but your female audience
will probably appreciate the extra verbiage. To her, you
sound a lot less tyrannical when you explain why you want
something.
- Then there are the requests that are perceived as unclear to
the man, yet perfectly clear to the woman. For example:
Shortly after taking my class on gender communication, a
man sent me this fabulous e-mail . . .

> Ronni,
> Thanks so much for a wonderful evening last
> night. My wife and I were out to dinner, and
> towards the end of the meal, she says to me,
> "Honey, I wonder where the ladies' room is?" Now,
> I had just come from your course on gender com-
> munication, and I knew that that meant some-
> thing, but I couldn't remember what. My usual
> response when she says things like that is some-
> thing like, "Why don't you ask someone—I bet
> they'll tell you." Then I thought, oh yeah, women
> don't ask for things directly; she wants me to find
> out where the ladies' room is. So I said, "Dear,
> would you like me to find out where the ladies'
> room is?" Sure enough, that's what she really
> wanted. I haven't seen her so pleased with me in a
> long time. We had a great night.
> Thanks again Ronni.

Alas, not all the emails I receive have happy endings.

- Wife asks husband, "Do I look too fat in these pants?"
Husband, thinking what he has learned says, "No Hon, you
look just fat enough." Oh Well.
- Men tend to interrupt more than women. They'll say "right" or
"okay" to let the speaker know that they understand what is

being said. Women, on the other hand, most often interrupt with something like "uh hum." It means the same thing.

Rent the Gary Shandling movie, *What Planet Are You From?* and you will see a beautiful example of this. An alien is sent to Earth to impregnate a woman and is told that women like to be listened to. The alien is instructed to respond, "uh huh" to anything women say. The movie is filled with stereotypical gender communication.

Remember that we are not here to make any judgments about who is correct or better. The point is to make the other person comfortable. So if you are a woman listening to a man, and you would like to interrupt, even if it is just to demonstrate that you understand, repress the urge to say "uh hum," and interject with a nice, firm "right." Remember who your audience is. *Cross address.*

- Men are more linear than women; they prefer to finish one story before beginning another. Women, on the other hand, are perfectly comfortable pursuing the numerous additional thoughts or stories that flow from whatever they are saying. When other women are their listeners, this is not a problem. However, men find this maddening. And because men have had less practice with this kind of organic conversation, they are often not as adept at it. As a result, they become frustrated because they cannot follow the speaker. If you are a woman speaking to a man, I suggest sticking to one thought at a time and following it to completion before beginning a new one. At the very least, make sure that you are listening and that your conversation has not become your monologue.

The Sound of Your Voice

- Women use a broader range of octaves when they speak. Their voices may swoop low and climb high all in one sentence. This often sounds either childlike or sing-songy. Either way, many women aren't taken seriously because of the sound of their voice. Meanwhile, men's voices tend to remain within a mid-to-low range and not deviate much. Listen to your recording of your voice and ask your buddy if it needs to be changed.
- Women speak at a faster pace than men. Meanwhile, men speak in a more choppy way than women, and that choppiness is often interpreted as abrupt, inapproachable, and even rude, *by women.*
- Women use pitch and inflection to emphasize points, while men use volume.

How You Listen

- Women sit directly in front of the person they are listening to, sit closer than a man would, and lean toward the speaker. Men tend to recline when listening, thereby creating more distance between themselves and those who are speaking.
- Women cock their head to the side and look at the speaker from an angle, while men look at the speaker with their heads straight, looking straight ahead at the speaker.
- Women use more body language when listening. They nod, open their eyes very wide, and provide more verbal feedback as well. Men, conversely, tend to squint their eyes when listening. It is easy to see how miscommunication occurs when men and women have almost opposite ways of demonstrating their listening and comprehension.

What You Look Like

- Men take up more physical space whether sitting or standing. They tend to stretch their arms and legs away from their bodies and they tend to move around more and shift their body position more. This creates the impression of power and dominance. Women, conversely, tend to curl up and keep their arms close to their bodies or crossed over their chests, and their legs or ankles crossed.
- Men gesture in a more forceful, choppy way than women do, and their gestures are usually directed away from their bodies. The gesturing of women tends to be more fluid, curvy, and toward their bodies. The best analogy is: man is to woman as karate is to ballet. These movements can be distracting, as gesturing should be kept to a minimum and should be meaningful.

The above information can go a long way to improving gender relations. Both men and women spend time interpreting the actions and words of others and making assumptions and conclusions based on those interpretations. If your interpretation is inaccurate, everything based on it will be inaccurate, as well. And the biggest error when interpreting the behavior of the opposite sex, is assessing it according to the standards and typical behavior of *your sex*. In other words, women shouldn't fault men for not being women, and they shouldn't be surprised when men don't behave and react the same way a woman would. Likewise for men.

Because the above list does not account for the uniqueness of the individual, I always strongly recommend clearing up any ambiguity by using the only technique that is foolproof. If you want to know what someone means by what they are saying, with their voice or otherwise, *ask*.

And if you want to develop rapport with someone, the sure way to begin is to assume their posture, adjust your breathing and your rate of speaking so it matches theirs, and take note of the language they like to use and incorporate it into your own verbiage. When you look, act, and speak like someone, you will actually begin to understand what they are feeling; you will begin to feel what they are feeling. You will have reached the state of empathy, and your communication will flow easily.

Summary

- Many aspects of the way men and women communicate are different. Those differences are a combination of nature and nurture, so some of them can be altered, while others cannot.
- Cross Addressing is bridging the gender gap by being sensitive to the gender of the person to whom you are speaking and presenting yourself and your ideas in a way that person (read: that gender) will be most receptive to.
- Some of the differences in the genders are:
  - Men tend to favor commands over requests
  - Women use more descriptive terms and intensifiers than men use.
  - Men favor definitive terms while women opt for less certain terms.
  - Women find the need to explain their requests, while men do not.
  - Men interrupt more than women do.
  - Women are less linear than men are in conversation, and speak faster.
  - Men tend to recline when listening, while women move closer to the speaker.
  - Women use more body language when listening.
  - Men gesture in a forceful, choppy way, while women gesture in a more fluid way.

Cross Addressing is another aspect of developing rapport. If you are a woman addressing a man, use language, gestures, and body language that are more stereotypically male in order to quickly develop rapport. And if you are a man addressing a woman, do the converse.

However, always keep in mind that we are each unique. Cross addressing should be enlisted only after you have observed that the person whom you are addressing has many characteristics typical of their gender. Use the clues the person is sending you, and communicate with them in a manner appropriate to those clues. They lead the dance.

CHAPTER EIGHT

Sarah and Simon:
A Sellabration of Awarenesss

Sarah and Simon are based on a gentleman who attended my seminar a short time ago and his wife, with whom he shared the information. They made a commitment to help each other become complete communicators by acting as buddies for each other. Warning: Your spouse or partner is not always the best choice for your buddy. Though your spouse or partner should be the obvious choice, the reality is that many couples are not comfortable with talking about communicating, particularly when it comes to anything remotely akin to critique. If you and your spouse/partner do not communicate well now, the exercises in this book can easily become a vehicle for criticism of all kinds, under the guise of *I'm just trying to help you!*

Remember that communication is about how a message is received, not how it was intended, so feedback is a crucial element in your journey of self-improvement.

Excerpts from Sarah and Simon's notebooks
*Note: As you read the excerpts, notice the difference between Sarah's entries and Simon's. Based on only the first couple of words, whose excerpts are they? After all of the entries, I'll discuss the differences further.

Self-Discovery #1: What You Say
Dear Notebook,

I was so busy all week that I didn't have time to listen to any of my tapes. I managed to carry the recorder around a lot, and it was such a pain at first, but after awhile it wasn't so bad. I felt a little like a secret agent at times. Other times I felt like I was doing something illegal.

Finally listened to the tapes, and I can't believe how many times I say "you know what I mean?" Sometimes it's just "know what I mean?" Then there are the times I start my sentences with "I mean ..."

All of this makes me sound like I'm not so sure I know what I mean. And for someone whose career involves a lot of public speaking, that can't be good.

Then there are the "uh's" that seem to dominate my phone calls. I never even hear them, but they are ubiquitous. It seems like every time I should be pausing, I say "uh" instead. And I draw it out, too; it's like "uuuuuhhhhhhhh." Not good.

Conversations with Simon were funny. He put on such a show when he thought he was being taped. Suddenly he became Articulate Man—Man of Perfectly Worded, Flawlessly Delivered Sentences. That's so not him. He made me so aware of his language that I became so aware of my language and I didn't sound like myself either. I sound much more self-conscious when I speak to him.

When we were talking about where we wanted to go in July, he had this perfect argument, used analogies, told me of how going to the South of France was more desirable than going to Bermuda to visit my friends, who just had another baby. He left me feeling really stupid for even thinking about wanting to go to Bermuda. I really felt like he was trying to sell me with all of his new techniques. His points were definitely valid, he presented me with a lot of the specific benefits to me of the France trip, and voila, we are going to France. But I didn't agree before I had a chance to tell him that I feel like he doesn't really listen to my side a lot of the time. France doesn't suck, so this really isn't a problem.

My presentations at work were fine. I'm good at answering questions on my feet, and I think I know the difference between what someone says and what they are feeling. Okay, so there are all of those "I mean's" that clearly can be eliminated. I did use a few words, like apoplectic and penultimate, that were probably not suitable for the audience.

Shopping was pretty funny. I had no idea how curt I am with salespeople. I don't even use full sentences. I have a tone of voice problem, too. I talk down to salespeople when I'm in a hurry or under stress. It doesn't really go with the smile—okay, fake smile—I probably had on my face.

I also learned that I talk to myself constantly when I am shopping. In fact, I talk to myself constantly when I am out of the house—out loud. And I amuse myself, too. I laugh all of the time; people must think I'm crazy.

Something interesting I've discovered is that I'm different to male salespeople—even more curt. What's up with that? And speaking of which, I say "What's up with that?" constantly. But other people do, as well. It sounds so silly on tape.

Simon says...

Simon tells me I sound like Elaine from Seinfeld. Funny because I said that he sounds like Jerry. He told me about the "know what I mean" thing, the "what's up with that" frequency, and my propensity for the long "uuhhhh." He makes me sound like Herman Munster the way he does the "uuuuhhhh." Apparently, I also say "cool," "really," and "groovy" a lot. How embarrassing.

Simon also said, once again, that he hates the way I order my food. As usual, I defended myself. Am I supposed to refrain from telling a waiter that I am allergic to garlic and I cannot eat dairy products? Am I supposed to eat my salad with all of that goop on it when I prefer to put on only as much as I want? He says that it's the way I do it that's a problem. He says I whine about it and ask if it's a problem and is it okay that I am allergic to garlic and don't want any? He says that we're paying for it, so I should just tell them exactly what I want. He thinks I should just say it; be direct.

Simon also thinks that my vocabulary is often "pretentious." He couldn't come up with any examples, and it wasn't really an insult, because he knows that I do have a better-than-average vocabulary. He says I should try to be more careful. "Remember who you're talking to," he tells me.

Self-Discovery #2: How You Sound

Boy do I sound whiny. All this time I thought I sounded like Lauren Bacall. It's more like Minnie Mouse, and I'm concerned. I have to try to lower my voice.

I'm also a lot more sarcastic than I thought I was. I made "Have a great day" sound obnoxious.

My presentations sound good, but I talk really fast at some points. When I lose my train of thought, I do this weird saliva-related thing that sounds like I'm sucking on a jawbreaker. It's like my mouth wants to be doing something all of the time. Although when I want to pause, that seems to go fine.

When I'm on the phone, I talk so fast, but it doesn't seem to bother anyone.

When I talk to people I don't know well, my voice is a lot lower and very polite sounding. But my natural speech sounds like a roller coaster. I do a lot more sound effects than I thought I did. I sound really dramatic on tape, especially when I talk to Simon.

When I talk to my friends from the South, where I grew up (in L.A.: Lower Alabama), I suddenly bust out into this southern accent. When I talk to my dad, who is a preacher, I'm super eloquent and I never cuss. When I talk to Simon, and only when I talk to Simon, I use many of *his* signature phrases, such as:

"tough break" (as in, I say, "Honey, would you please pass me the milk?" to which he responds, "I just drank the last drop—tough break");

"no chance" (as in "Honey, would you please pass me the milk?" at which time he begins to, but when I reach for it, he pulls it back and says, "No chance");

"best of luck to you," which is more like "bestalucktoya," and has multiple meanings, all of which are sarcastic.

I find these phrases so annoying when he says them (constantly), yet there I am stealing his most irritating Simon-isms. How ironic. How embarrassing.

Simon says...
Simon says I talk too fast all of the time. He likes my sarcasm, but calls me a lightweight and insists I'm not nearly as clever as he is, but that it's not my fault that I was born in Alabama (typical New Yorker—even sarcastic about sarcasm).

Simon says I'm one of the funniest people he knows. He says I'm like a female Steve Martin at his wackiest. Cool.

Simon complains that when I talk to him on the phone, he can't hear me. I've heard that before. Apparently I speak low, softly, and I mumble. What a combo. I think I'm lazy when on the phone. I have to start speaking up.

Self-Discovery #3: How You Listen
I didn't think I'd be able to hear anything that would tell me how I listened, but I actually did get an idea. I think I'm pretty good. I guess I really did learn something from the years I spent in psychotherapy. I say "uh huh" and "I understand" and "I see" when I get what's going on, and I do chime in with an occasional "would you please explain that" and "I'm not sure I understand" when I don't.

No one said anything like "would you just listen to me" or "would you let me speak," like I have to say to Simon all of the time, so I assume I'm doing okay. Cool.

Simon says...
Simon reminded me that one of the reasons he married me is that I am a good listener. His only complaint, which I hear a lot, is that I say "I know" a lot, and that from his observations, I do that only with him. After the first time he told me of his complaint, I started saying "really?" and then he told me I sounded like I was playing dumb. I stopped with the "reallys." I can't win. I tell him that it's not my fault

that I know a lot of stuff, and when he comes up with something new, I'll let him know.

Self-Discovery #4: How You Look

What I could tell from the recording is that I move my arms a lot for emphasis. I know that because it created a lot of noise on the tape.

Simon says...

Well, he had a gas doing this part. He really entertained himself trying to mimic all of my gestures and the way I talk. Then he proceeded to what he calls, The Sarah Series, which is a group of faces that I commonly use when I am talking and when I am listening. I refuse to believe that they are as exaggerated as his impersonations, but I do admit that I occasionally enlist some choice facial expressions to help me tell a story.

Simon says I don't realize how animated I am. He thinks it's "cute," which is a euphemism for I look like a moron. When I got over being insulted, he did give me a few pointers. He told me of the part in Ronni's seminar where she talks about using your hands. Apparently I use my hands a lot, and the movements usually have nothing to do with what I'm saying. After Simon shows me what my hands look like, he says "let me put it this way, you look like you are trying to strangle a tree, but there's no tree."

Simon came to one of my presentations at work and says he was amazed at how different I am. He says, "you look so professional and so comfortable up there. Your eye contact is good, you are sincere, you listen to the questions put to you and thoughtfully reply, even though you and I both know that you don't have to think much to answer those stupid questions, and you're funny up there." Great, I say to myself, I'm home free on this one. Then he says, "Do you clasp your hands behind your back to prevent them from flailing and strangling trees?"

Everybody's a comedian. I guess I have to work on the hand thing.

Oh, and he told me that he wished I could be so calm and pleasant when I talk to him. I told him that would be easy if he would stop making a career out of pushing my buttons. "But you make it so easy, Sarah! I can't resist!" I told him it's not a tree I'm strangling.

Self-Discovery #5a: Humor

I like to think that I can find humor in anything. But I find humor in everything. Now I know why my mother constantly complains that I don't take anything seriously. But it's different with her. I know when I'm supposed to be serious with her, but I just can't help making a joke or saying something sarcastic. Personally, I think she should just lighten up.

One of the conversations I taped was an exchange with my mother at lunch. I was complaining that Simon constantly makes fun of me. She calls it "justice," and says that she knows exactly how I feel because I do the exact same thing to her. I guess she's right. I felt like Simon must feel when I yell at him for mocking me.

Mom did, however, tell me how funny she thinks I am. She uses the Steve Martin analogy, too. She also tells me I remind her of the actress Holly Hunter and Elaine from Seinfeld. I consider all of it complimentary, although all three are quite neurotic.

Simon says...

Simon says I'm "a hoot and a holler." You'd think he was the one from Alabama. He says my sense of humor is the other reason why he married me. Let's reiterate, shall we? He married me because I listen to him and I entertain him. Glad to be of service.

Simon and I went to the movie rental place and, separately, we made lists of the movies we wanted to rent. The deal is that, each week, we rent one of mine and one of his. It sounded like a good idea until I saw his list. How many times can one person sit through *Blazing Saddles* and *Monty Python's Life of Brian*? And is *Dumb and Dumber* really that funny? I guess I too am going to have memorized the script when this is all over.

Self-Discovery #5b: Intuition

I have such a head start in this category. Despite my dad being a preacher, it was my mom who really raised us, and she is a Buddhist. Add that to the fact that reading about quantum physics is my hobby, and I don't have a problem in this area.

Not only do I know how to interpret my bodily cues, but I have a system that makes my dreams virtually transparent. I have learned that the more I question what I am feeling, the greater the probability that I will screw up as a result. I can't explain it (obviously); I just go with it and it works.

When I first met Simon, I had a feeling about him. It wasn't love at first sight or anything, but for some reason, I just knew that I should sit back and watch him flounder a bit, on his timetable, and be his friend. So I did. A couple of months later, we both came to the realization, simultaneously, that we were meant for each other. We never had a doubt and we never looked back. It sounds so corny, but it's true.

I get the same feeling when I meet new clients. Sometimes. When I get the feeling, I pursue a relationship with them. When I get this other feeling I get, which isn't so pleasant, I don't take them on as clients.

Simon says...

Simon says he is in awe of my intuition. For years I've been trying to tell him that mine is no better than his, and the sooner he gets acquainted with his, the better off he'll be. I think he's finally taking this seriously.

Self-Discovery #5c:Creative Thinking

People often tell me that I think "outside-the-box." It's true, and in fact I'm quite proud of my unconventional ways. From a young age, my curiosity was never hindered by my parents or teachers. I was an artistic child, a musical child, a dancer, and I had a passion for math. I never felt self-conscious when I didn't know something, because I was confident that I could either figure it out myself, or find someone to help me.

Simon says...

Simon says that sometimes I am so outside the box that I don't see that the conventional way might be the easiest way. It's hardly as fun for me, though.

Simon thinks I should spend more time doing sports. He suggests golf. He says I'll like it because it's such a mental game and I'm such a mental person (it was supposed to be a compliment, but it didn't sound like one). He says it'll make me an even better thinker. I've heard that. Maybe I'll try it.

Excerpts from Simon's notebook
What you say

1. Words to say less often:
   Best of luck to you, No chance, Tough Break, How did that work out for you?
   Fantastic
   Sweet
   There you go
   I've got that going for me
2. Stop saying "um."
3. Practice pausing.
4. Don't phrase your opinions like they're facts.
5. Stop quoting *Caddyshack, Fletch*, and *A Few Good Men*. Sometimes people have no clue you're doing it.
6. Sarah said all of the above, too. Also—I am not as polite as I could be and I sometimes sound abrupt. She says I should try to say please and thank you more. No chance.

How you say it

1. Stop barking commands.
2. Lower the volume of your voice. Sounds like you're always yelling.
3. Lose the New York accent.
4. Stop doing the heavy sigh when you are frustrated. Sounds bratty.
5. Very sarcastic. Might want to decrease that. Or not.

How you listen

1. Stop interrupting.
2. Replace "I hear ya" with something. Anything.
3. Practice pausing.
4. Talk less—I do most of the talking
5. Sarah says I don't listen. She says things like would you just listen to me—a lot. She says I don't let her get a word in and that I interrupt her all of the time.

What you look like

Asked some people at work, and they all said the same stuff Sarah said.

1. I don't use my hands a lot.
2. The only facial expression they point out is the one that makes them feel like they just said something I think is stupid. They all tried to make the face. Some were pretty good.
3. I stare at people when I talk to them, and it makes them uncomfortable. Sometimes it makes them think I'm not even really seeing them. They tell me I appear to be looking through them. Tough break.
4. I sit with my legs spread apart and Sarah says it's gross.

Humor

1. Women think some of my humor is gross. They say I'm such a guy. I get a lot of eyeball rolls from women. Men haven't complained.
2. My sarcasm gets eye rolls, too. Sarah says did you have to say that? Sometimes I can't resist. It's all in fun. She should lighten up. It is really starting to annoy her.
3. We now rent two movies every week; one that she likes, one that I like. We like a lot of the same stuff, but the differences are huge and she acts like my sense of humor is beneath her sometimes. That just makes me want to act even more gross.

Intuition

1. The other day I got butterflies in my stomach when I was driving. I turned where I don't usually turn. Nothing happened. Sarah says maybe if I didn't turn something would have happened.

2. I get these déjà vu flashes. Or at least it seems like déjà vu. Somehow I just do what I know I'm supposed to do. It drives me crazy when I think about why things like that happen.

3. People tell me I have good instincts about people—whether they're trustworthy or not. I've never been wrong. When I first meet people I just get a feeling about them and go with it. I don't look for it; it just happens.

4. I started looking for signs. I wonder what's a sign and what isn't. Or what's a sign for me—what am I supposed to be responding to? Sarah says this is how to drive myself crazy, for sure.

Creative Thinking

1. Sarah says I have to break out of the box—that my thinking is very predictable and lazy. That's probably true. I call it common sense.

2. I play a lot of sports, do a lot of daydreaming. I don't do anything artistic. Sarah and I talk about designing a garden together. I wonder if that counts as art.

3. Tried driving to work using a different route, then I went on a five mile run that was totally different than any other run. I remember everything about both. Even smells. Both the drive and the run seemed like they took a real long time, though.

4. At work, I thought about how I approached every situation that could have been a problem, and I did come up with alternatives. They were just theoretical—couldn't bring myself to try something new when the thing I always do works. Maybe alternatives would work even better, though.

Conclusion

Complete communicators actively pursue three things: understanding themselves, understanding other people, and being understood. As such, complete communicators are mindful of all of the factors that affect understanding and being understood. They are aware of themselves and others during any communication. Most people have to work at that.

After years of working as a spokesperson, a salesperson, and a consultant, my experience is that there are very few people who *don't* have room for improvement in the way they communicate in the business world. And as a daughter, a mother (of a boy), and a wife, I am constantly aware of the impact of miscommunication, the dynamics of male-female communication, and the need for more awareness and sensitivity to differences.

The Golden Rule

Complete communicators live according to The Golden Rule of Communication: Do unto others *as they would have you do unto them.* As a result, the starting point for what you will say, how you will say it, how you will listen, and how you will look, is always the other person. *The other person leads the dance.*

Following the cues of the other person means that you are attentive to the way they talk, the way they breathe, and the way they carry themselves. It means you listen for their pet phrases and the kinds of things they find funny. It means you take their gender into account when you interact with them. It means you *cross address*, and respect the way your different-gender listener likes to be spoken to.

The more comfortable someone is with you, the more likely they are to listen to you, to *hear* you, and to receive to your ideas. And the best way to make someone comfortable is to present yourself and your ideas in a way that is not threatening to them. Fortunately, they are giving you plenty of signals that tell you how they want to be treated.

All you have to do is pay attention, and act accordingly. The way people communicate is often a clue about how they want you to communicate with them.

Act accordingly does not mean you change who you are or what you mean. It simply means you should mirror the other person as much as possible because we tend to like people who are like us. Act accordingly means creating an environment where the other person feels at ease. Think about it this way: Would you want to listen to someone if they were making you uncomfortable?

The best salespeople I know are also the best communicators I know. The reason is that those salespeople have tapped into the source of all successful communication: they pay attention to all of the signals the customer is giving them, and then they give the customer what they want. And I'm not talking about the products or services that they want, I am talking about the way they want to be treated. The goal for successful salespeople is mutual satisfaction.

Be What You Mean

Each of us is a walking, talking message. Our words tell a story. But the qualities of our voice affect that story and can easily alter it. And our facial expression, our gesturing, and even our posture, affect our story profoundly. Therefore, our words and our original intentions are meaningless unless our voice and body language are telling the same story. Consistency among all of the aspects of communication will help your intention become the message that is received. Consistency will help you reach complete communication.

Your Journey Toward Complete Communication

The best way to achieve any goal is to have a plan for how to get there. Complete communication is a goal that you can work toward by improving each of its components, one at a time. The components are:

- What you say

- How you say it

- How you listen

- What you look like

- The *invisible* elements—humor, intuition, and creative thinking

The way to improve these components, or any other aspect of your behavior, is to first establish where you are right now. I recommended enlisting the help of your buddy and a microcassette recorder; you may have used a different method (and I'd like to hear all about it). The purpose of whichever method you used, was to get a feel for how the rest of the world sees you. You know how you see yourself and how you think other people see you, but you don't know how others see you until you ask and until you are able to see yourself as they do. (Videotape is optimal, but unrealistic. If you ever get the opportunity to take a course or be coached and be videotaped, it's worth it. The tape will show you what very few people can fully explain to you.)

You Are In Control

When you look through your five-subject notebook, you will find that you are a predictable creature. We all are. You have developed a vocabulary and a way of communicating (verbally and nonverbally) that is a result of a number of factors, including: your geographical location, your profession, your education, your age, your gender, and your outlook on life. Some of those factors involve choices (e.g., your profession, your outlook, your education, whom you socialize with), while others do not (i.e., your age, the region you grew up in).

Unfortunately, many people spend most of their time acting like *their lives are something that happen to them*. The journey toward complete communication involves the realization that you have control over a lot more of your behavior than you might have previously thought. You can control the message your body sends, you can control your thoughts, and you can control your creative thinking. You can even train yourself to call upon your intuition when you need to.

The catch is that assuming control of your life is a big responsibility. When you realize that much of your life is your own creation, you become the party accountable for the results—not God, not your mother, you.

So if you'd like to change anything about the results you've been getting in your relationships at home or at work, you have to change your approach. Remember that adage used so frequently in the motivation industry: If you do what you've always done, you'll get what you always got. You are perfectly positioned to change the outcome of your communication; it is a decision.

READINGS AND RESOURCES

Ayan, Jordan. *Aha! 10 Ways to Free Your Creative Spirit and Find Your Great Ideas.* New York: Three Rivers, 1997.

Bandler, Richard. *Frogs into Prices: Neuro Linguistic Programming.* Moab, UT: Real People Press, 1979.

—— and John Grinder. *The Structure of Magic I & II.* Palo Alto, CA: Science and Behavior Books, 1976.

——. *Reframing: Neuro Linguistic Programming and the Transformation of Meaning.* Moab, UT: Real People Press, 1982.

Berkley, Susan. *Speak to Influence: How to Unlock the Hidden Power of Your Voice.* Englewood Cliffs, NJ: Campbell Hall, 1999.

Berra, Yogi, et al. *"I Really Didn't Say Everything I Said."* New York: Workman, 1988.

Birdwhistell, Ray L. *Kinesics and Context: Essays on Body Motion Communication.* Philadelphia: University of Pennsylvania, 1970.

Brooks, Michael, Dr. *The Power of Business Rapport: Use NLP Technology to Make More Money, Sell Yourself and Your Product, and Move Ahead in Business.* New York: Harper Collins, 1991.

Burley-Allen, Madelyn. *Listening: The Forgotten Skill.* New York: Wiley, 1995.

Buzan, Tony. *Make the Most of Your Mind.* New York: Simon and Schuster, 1984.

Canary, Daniel and Tara Emmers-Sommer. *Sex and Gender Differences in Personal Relationships.* London: Guilford, 1997.

Cialdini, Robert B., Ph.D. *Influence: The New Psychology of Modern Persuasion.* New York:William Morrow, 1985.

Cohen, Herb. *You Can Negotiate Anything.* New York: Bantam, 1982.

Cousins, Norman. *Head First: The Biology of Hope and the Healing Power of the Human Spirit.* New York: Penguin Putnam, 1990.

Covey, Steven R. *The 7 Habits of Highly Effective People.* New York: Simon and Schuster, 1990.

De Bono, Edward. *Edward De Bono's Thinking Course.* New York:

Facts on File, 1994.

———. *Six Thinking Hats*. New York: Little, Brown, 1985.

DePorter, Bobbi. *Quantum Learning: Unleashing the Genius in You.* New York:, Dell, 1992.

Dimitrius, Jo-Ellan, Ph.D. and Mark Mazzarella. *Reading People: How to Understand People And Predict Their Behavior Anytime, Anyplace.* New York: Random House, 1998.

Donovan, Priscilla and Jacquelyn Wonder. *Whole Brain Thinking: Working from Both Sides of the Brain to Achieve Peak Job Performance.* New York: William Morrow, 1984.

Ekman, Paul. *Telling Lies: Clues to Deceit in the Marketplace, Politics, and Marriage.* New York: W.W. Norton and Co., 1992

Ellis, Albert, Ph.D. and Robert A. Harper, Ph..D. *A Guide to Rational Living.* North Hollywood, CA: Wilshire, 1997.

Emerick, John J., Jr., *Be the Person You Want to Be: Harness the Power of Neuro Linguistic Programming to Reach Your Potential.* Rocklin, CA: Prima, 1997.

Fay, Allen, M.D. *Making Things Better by Making Them Worse.* New York: Hawthorne, 1978.

Gardner, Howard. *Frames of Mind: The Theory of Multiple Intelligences.* Basic Books, 1983.

Glass, Lillian, Ph.D. *He Says, She Says: Closing the Communication Gap Between the Sexes.* New York: Perigree, 1992.

Hartman, Taylor, Ph.D. *The Color Code: A New Way to See Yourself, Your Relationships, and Life.* New York: Simon and Schuster, 1987.

Hayakawa, S. I. *Language in Thought and Action.* New York: Harcourt Brace Javanovich, 1972.

Herd., John H., and Donald J. Moine. *Modern Persuasion Strategies: The Hidden Advantage of Selling.* Englewood Cliffs, NJ: Prentice Hall, 1984.

Hogan, Kevin. *The Psychology of Persuasion: How to Persuade Others to Your Way of Thinking.* Gretna, LA: Pelican, 1996.

Horn, Sam. *Tongue Fu! How to Deflect, Disarm, and Defuse Any Verbal Conflict.* New York: St. Martin's Griffin, 1996.

Inner Knowing. Ed. Helen Palmer. New York: Penguin Putnam, 1998.

Klein, Allen. *The Healing Power of Humor.* New York: Penguin Putnam, 1976.

LaBorde, Genie. *Influencing with Integrity: Management Skills for Communication and Negotiation.* Palo Alto, CA: Syntony, 1984.

———. *Fine Tune Your Brain: Management Skills for Communication and Negotiation.* Palo Alto, CA: Syntony, 1988.

Langer, Ellen. *Mindfulness. Reading,* Massachusetts: Perseus, 1990.

MacKenzie, Gordon. *Orbiting the Giant Hairball: A Corporate Fool's Guide to Surviving With Grace.* New York: Viking Penguin, 1998.

Mehrabian, Albert. *Silent Messages: Implicit Communication of Emotions and Attitudes.* Belmont, CA: Wadsworth, 1981.

Metcalf, C.W. and Roma Felible. *Lighten Up: Survival Skills for People Under Stress.* Reading, Massachusetts: Perseus, 1992.

Morris, Desmond. *The Naked Ape: A Zoologist's Study of the Human Animal.* New York: Dell, 1999.

Nichols, Michael P., Ph.D. *The Lost Art of Listening: How Learning to Listen Can Improve Relationships.* New York: Guilford, 1995.

Peale, Norman Vincent. *Positive Thinking Every Day.* New York: Simon and Schuster, 1993.

Ries, Al and Jack Trout. *Positioning: The Battle for Your Mind.* New York: McGraw Hill, 1986.

Ritberger, Carol, Ph.D. *What Color is Your Personality?* Carlsbad, CA: Hay House, 2000.

Satir, Virginia. *New Peoplemaking.* Palo Alto, CA: Science and Behavior Books, 1976.

Seligman, Martin, Ph.D. *Learned Optimism.* New York: Pocket, 1990.

Spoelstra, Joe. *Success is Just One Wish Away.* Las Vegas: DelStar, 1998.

Von Oech, Roger, Ph.D. *A Whack on the Side of the Head: How You Can Be More Creative.* New York: Warner, 1983.

——. *A Kick in the Seat of the Pants: Using Your Explorer, Artist, Judge, and Warrior to be More Creative.* New York: Harper Perennial, 1986.

Wilson, Larry. *Changing the Game: The New Way to Sell.* New York: Fireside, 1987.

Made in the USA
Charleston, SC
04 December 2012